CAMPAIGN 291

THE DNEPR 1943

Hitler's eastern rampart crumbles

ROBERT FORCZYK

ILLUSTRATED BY STEVE NOON

Series editor Marcus Cowper

First published in Great Britain in 2016 by Osprey Publishing,
PO Box 883, Oxford, OX1 9PL, UK
PO Box 3985, New York, NY 10185-3985, USA
E-mail: info@ospreypublishing.com

A CIP catalogue record for this book is available from the British Library.

ISBN: 978 1 4728 1237 7
PDF e-book ISBN: 978 14728 1238 4
e-Pub ISBN: 978 14728 1239 1

Editorial by Ilios Publishing Ltd, Oxford, UK (www.iliospublishing.com)
Index by Alison Worthington
Typeset in Myriad Pro and Sabon
Maps by Bounford.com
3D bird's-eye views by The Black Spot
Battlescene illustrations by Steve Noon
Originated by PDQ Media, Bungay, UK
Printed in China through Worldprint Ltd.

16 17 18 19 20   10 9 8 7 6 5 4 3 2 1

ARTIST'S NOTE

Readers may care to note that the original paintings from which the colour
plates in this book were prepared are available for private sale. The
Publishers retain all reproduction copyright whatsoever. The artist can be
contacted via the following website:
www.steve-noon.co.uk
The Publishers regret that they can enter into no correspondence upon this
matter.

THE WOODLAND TRUST

Osprey Publishing are supporting the Woodland Trust, the UK's leading
woodland conservation charity, by funding the dedication of trees.

LIST OF ACRONYMS AND ABBREVIATIONS

AOK	Armeeoberkommando (Army Command)
GCC	Guards Cavalry Corps
GRD	Guards Rifle Division
GRC	Guards Rifle Corps
JG	Jagdgeschwader
HKL	Hauptkampflinie (main line of resistance)
KG	Kampfgeschwader
KIA	Killed in action
LSSAH	1.SS-Panzer-Division Leibstandarte SS Adolf Hitler
NKO	Narodny Komissariat Oborony (People's Commissariat of Defence)
NKVD	Narodnyy Komissariat Vnutrennikh Del (People's Commissariat of Internal Affairs)
OKH	Oberkommando des Heeres
PzKpfw	Panzerkampfwagen
SchG	Schlachtgeschwader
SPW	Schützenpanzerwagen
StG	Sturzkampfgeschwader
StuG	Sturmgeschütz
VVS	Voyenno-Vozdushnye Sily (Military Air Forces)

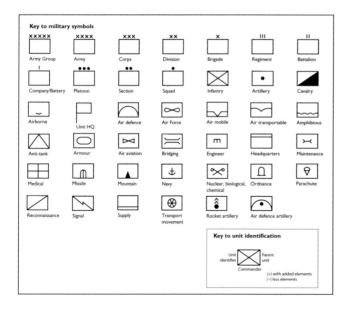

CONTENTS

ORIGINS OF THE CAMPAIGN

The Germans re-opened the repaired railway bridge over the Dnepr at Zaporozhe in June 1942, but some of the bridges over the Dnepr were not repaired until early 1943. All were blown up by the retreating Germans in autumn 1943. (Author's collection)

After the German 6.Armee was surrounded at Stalingrad in November 1942, the war in the East swung inexorably against the Third Reich. Due to this catastrophe, the entire German effort in southern Russia and the Caucasus was compromised and Generalfeldmarschall Erich von Manstein was rushed in to handle the crisis. While containing the 6.Armee, other Soviet armies advanced towards Rostov and Kharkov, demolishing the Italian Eighth Army in the process. Von Manstein succeeded in cobbling together Heeresgruppe Don, but he was unable to save the doomed 6.Armee or to stop the relentless Soviet advance westwards. By mid-February 1943, General Nikolai Vatutin's Voronezh Front had liberated Kharkov and Soviet tanks were within 30km of the Dnepr River. The Red Army appeared to be on the cusp of a major strategic victory that would decide the war in the East. However, von Manstein received strong armoured reinforcements from the West just in time, which allowed him to recapture Kharkov and defeat the overextended Soviet armoured spearheads before they reached the Dnepr. Both sides suffered enormous material and personnel losses during January–March 1943 that left them exhausted; the Germans lost 2,152 tanks and the Soviets 5,023.

A period of relative calm settled over the Eastern Front for three months during April–June 1943, with both sides refitting their forces and preparing for the next round. The Oberkommando des Heeres (OKH) prioritised replacements for von Manstein's command, redesignated Heeresgruppe Süd, which enabled him to re-establish a strong defensive front from the Sea of Azov north to Belgorod. Many of the battered German Panzer divisions were rebuilt, up to at least 50–80 per cent of authorised strength, giving von Manstein a total of over 1,500 tanks and assault guns. Yet the Red Army was also rebuilding and growing much stronger, in both numerical and qualitative terms, which made von Manstein's efforts little more than a stopgap. At this point in spring 1943, Hitler and the OKH had to make a crucial strategic decision about the future conduct of the war in the East. From the purely military perspective, the best course of action was to create a large, mobile Panzer reserve

German trucks retreat across the Dnepr River, while civilians march alongside the columns. The Germans forced thousands of civilians and their livestock to relocate west of the Dnepr to deny them to the Red Army. (Author's collection)

with the rebuilt divisions to defeat future Soviet offensives and to remain on the defensive, hoping to bleed the enemy dry. This course of action also suggested that Germany should create strong defences behind the Dnepr River as a fallback position, since this natural obstacle could serve as a moat against the Soviet tank armies. However, Hitler was averse to defensive strategies in the East or to creating fixed defensive lines, which he thought would encourage his generals to abandon territory too easily. He also wanted to retain vulnerable but economically important areas such as the coal and iron ore deposits in the Donbass. Thus, Hitler rejected the notion of fortifying the Dnepr River and instead gambled that another offensive could regain the initiative in the East.

The Germans tried to destroy the railroads as they retreated in order to slow the Soviet pursuit. Soviet logistic capabilities in September 1943 were still heavily tied to rail lines due to the shortage of trucks; the ability of the Red Army's engineers to repair damaged rail lines was also insufficient, which meant that it would take many weeks before the Soviets were capable of sustaining large-scale operations west of the Dnepr. (Courtesy of the Central Museum of the Armed Forces, Moscow via Stavka)

The Schienenwolf ('Track Wolf') was developed in 1942 and used a Krupp-built steel plough to break the wooden sleepers, thereby making the rail line unusable. Two locomotives were required to pull the plough and it could move up to 7–10km in one hour. This was a relatively effective and quick method of disabling rail lines, supplemented by demolition of rail stations and bridges. (Nik Cornish at www.Stavka.org.uk)

At Hitler's direction, the OKH developed a plan to conduct a pincer attack against the Soviet-held Kursk salient with von Manstein's Heeresgruppe Süd and Generalfeldmarschall Günther von Kluge's Heeresgruppe Mitte. Massing the bulk of the best mechanised and air units against the Kursk salient, Hitler believed that Operation *Zitadelle* would inflict massive losses on the Red Army and thereby purchase time for Germany to regain its military strength. However, the Soviet Stavka (high command) easily anticipated the German offensive and opted to heavily fortify the salient with unprecedented amounts of mines, anti-tank guns and tanks. When the German offensive began on 5 July 1943, it quickly became apparent that surprise had been lost and *Zitadelle* degenerated into a costly battle of attrition. Although Generaloberst Hermann Hoth's 4.Panzerarmee was able to advance 38km and inflict 90,000 casualties upon Vatutin's Voronezh Front and Ivan Konev's Steppe Front, von Manstein's forces never came close to reaching Kursk, their operational objective. Furthermore, *Zitadelle* rendered two-thirds of Heeresgruppe Süd's armour inoperative due to battle damage and mechanical defects. Consequently, Hitler decided to cancel *Zitadelle* on 13 July and shift to the defensive. However, the Red Army had no intention of allowing the Germans to recover from their failure at Kursk.

Only two days after Heeresgruppe Mitte suspended its attack against the northern side of the Kursk salient, the Soviet Central, Western and Bryansk fronts commenced their own massive counter-offensive known as Operation *Kutuzov*. Four days after *Zitadelle* was cancelled, General Fyodor I. Tolbukhin's Southern Front

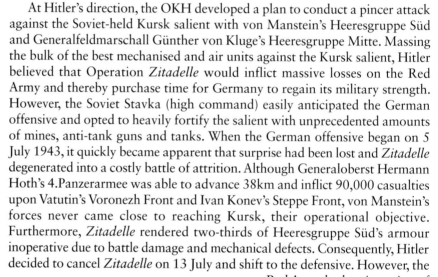

Hitler ordered Heeresgruppe Süd to employ 'scorched earth' tactics as it retreated through the Ukraine. Here, German troops leave a Ukrainian village in flames. Such tactics led to looting and other breakdowns of discipline within the retreating German units. (Author's collection)

The situation in the Ukraine, 15 September 1943.

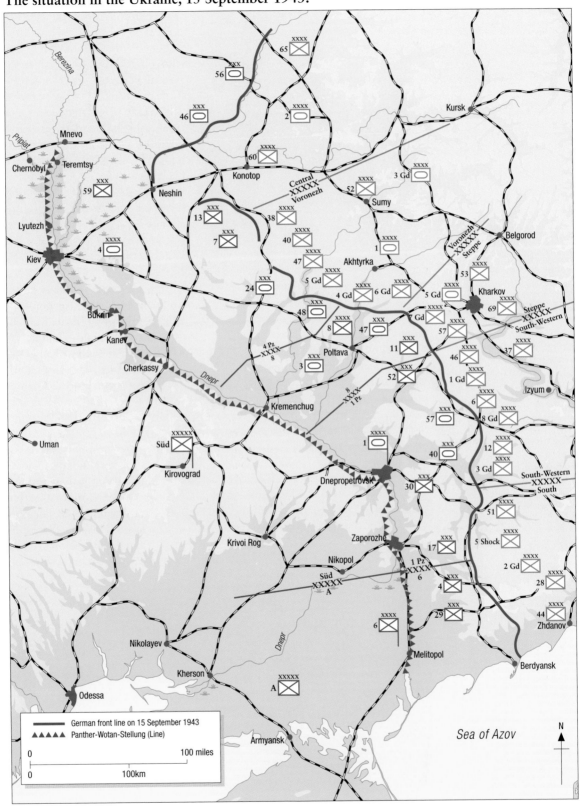

A Soviet truck passes an abandoned German sFH 18 15cm howitzer and its prime mover. Heeresgruppe Süd lost a great deal of artillery and equipment during the retreat to the Dnepr, which degraded its ability to conduct defensive operations. (Author's collection)

launched a major attack against the rebuilt 6.Armee and gained a deep bridgehead across the Mius River. Von Manstein was compelled to transfer both II SS-Panzerkorps and XXIV Panzerkorps to contain Tolbukhin's bridgehead and conduct a major counter-offensive on 30 July. After four days of heavy fighting, Tolbukhin's bridgehead was demolished, but it was a costly tactical victory that further reduced von Manstein's already depleted Panzer divisions. Just as that crisis passed, Vatutin's Voronezh Front and Konev's Steppe Front commenced Operation *Rumyantsev* on 3 August, which shattered the front of Hoth's 4.Panzerarmee west of Belgorod. The Soviet 1st Tank Army and 5th Guards Tank Army were pushed into the breach and drove a deep wedge into von Manstein's front line, and Belgorod fell on 5 August. With great difficulty, von Manstein managed to assemble his remaining armour west of Kharkov and fought the two Soviet tank armies to a standstill between the towns of Akhtyrka and Bogodukhov. Nevertheless, Heeresgruppe Süd's front was beginning to crack and Konev liberated Kharkov on 23 August. Another brief period of stalemate ensued as both sides replenished their losses and supplies, but it was increasingly clear to von Manstein after the fall of Kharkov that Heeresgruppe Süd could no longer hold its positions in eastern Ukraine. Between 1 July and 10 September 1943, the four armies within Heeresgruppe Süd suffered over 180,000 casualties, including 49,269 dead or missing. General der Infanterie Otto Wöhler's 8.Armee was the hardest hit, accounting for one-third of von Manstein's total losses. Those of the infantry were particularly crippling, making it difficult to hold a continuous front line, but tank losses were also severe.

German trucks and horse-drawn vehicles crossing a minor stream during the retreat to the Dnepr. Rear-echelon units bolted for the Dnepr, one step ahead of the pursuing Soviets. (Author's collection)

Despite these series of defeats in July and August, Hitler refused to discuss withdrawals. He did approve creation of the Panther-Stellung (line) behind the Dnepr, but still hoped that von Manstein would stop the Soviet offensives without having to retreat. Instead, the Soviet Voronezh, Steppe, South-Western and Southern fronts continued to pound Heeresgruppe Süd during the first week of September, further chipping away at von Manstein's remaining infantry

German troops wait in a defensive position alongside a road, while wheeled transport heads west. Note the Faustpatrone (Panzerfaust 30 kleine) anti-tank launcher between the two infantrymen. This early version of the Panzerfaust was just reaching front-line troops in September 1943 but was not yet available in the quantities that would be evident in 1944–45. In any case, covering units like this could only delay the Soviet pursuit for the briefest of periods. (Nik Cornish at www.Stavka.org.uk)

and tanks. Malinovsky's South-Western Front launched an attack out of its Izyum bridgehead over the Donets, which severely stressed 1.Panzerarmee, while Tolbukhin renewed his offensive over the Mius River against 6.Armee. In late August, the 2nd Guards Army achieved a major breakthrough near Stalino which isolated one of 6.Armee's corps against the Sea of Azov. Through aggressive counter-attacks, the German corps managed to break out but 6.Armee's front was near collapse. On 2 September, General Konstantin K. Rokossovsky's Central Front, which had eliminated the Orel salient, broke through Heeresgruppe Mitte's right flank at Sumy. Rokossovsky's forces could either roll up Hoth's left flank, head straight to Kiev, or do both. With no reserves left to seal the breach between Heeresgruppe Mitte and Heeresgruppe Süd, it suddenly became clear even to Hitler that there was no choice but to retreat – yet he delayed making the decision for almost another two weeks.

Rybalko's 3rd Guards Tank Army loaded up infantrymen on each tank and headed south-west to the Dnepr in pursuit of the retreating Germans. When the tanks ran out of fuel short of the Dnepr, the sub-machine gunners dismounted and walked the last few miles to the river. (Courtesy of the Central Museum of the Armed Forces, Moscow via Stavka)

On 6 September, Tolbukhin's forces achieved a major breakthrough and liberated Stalino two days later. Two Soviet mobile corps, the 1st Guards Mechanised Corps and the 23rd Tank Corps, advanced westwards to Pavlograd, which was within 40km of Dnepropetrovsk. Between 9 and 11 September, the Germans scraped together enough tanks to launch a counter-attack that temporarily isolated the two Soviet mobile corps, but they lacked the strength to destroy them. Consequently, 6.Armee was in danger of being encircled and destroyed between Tolbukhin's and Malinovsky's forces. With von Manstein's right flank crumbling and his left flank being turned, Hitler finally authorised von Manstein to retreat to the Dnepr on 15 September.

The wide Dnepr River offered the only possible refuge which might afford Heeresgruppe Süd a strong enough defensible position to stabilise a new front line. However, von Manstein's depleted forces would have to retreat to the river with the Red Army in hot pursuit, providing very little time to create a continuous defence. Five Soviet fronts were involved in the subsequent Lower Dnepr campaign, making it one of the Red Army's largest offensive operations of World War II, involving over 2 million troops. The outcome of the Lower Dnepr campaign would decide the war in the East. If the Germans could build a viable Eastern rampart behind the river, a stalemate of sorts might still be achievable; if not, the Third Reich was finished.

CHRONOLOGY

1943

13 July	Hitler suspends Operation *Zitadelle*.
30 July–2 August	Operation *Roland* (German) on the Mius River.
11 August	Hitler authorises creation of the Panther-Stellung.
23 August	Konev's Steppe Front liberates Kharkov.
15 September	Hitler authorises von Manstein to withdraw to the Panther-Stellung behind the Lower Dnepr River.
19 September	Rybalko's 3rd Guards Tank Army begins advancing towards the Dnepr.
20 September	19.Panzer-Division crosses to the west side of the Dnepr at Kiev. The 13th Army from Central Front establishes a first bridgehead across the Dnepr near Teremtsy.
21 September	Lead tanks from the 3rd Guards Tank Army approach the Dnepr Bend.
22 September	The 3rd Guards Tank Army and 40th Army establish bridgeheads across the Dnepr near Bukrin.
20–23 September	III and XXXXVIII Panzerkorps fight a delaying action at Poltava.
24 September	The Soviet airborne operation near Kanev fails, as does an attempt to break out of the Bukrin bridgehead.
25 September	Konev's forces cross the Dnepr at Uspenka.
26 September	The first Soviet tanks begin crossing the Dnepr (3rd Guards Tank Army). Tolbukhin's forces begin a major assault against 6.Armee at Melitopol.
27 September	Konev's forces cross the Dnepr at Deriyivka.
28 September	The 38th Army seizes a small bridgehead at Lyutezh, north of Kiev.
1 October	The 13th Army liberates Chernobyl and gains a bridgehead over the Pripiat River.
2 October	Konev expands his small bridgeheads and captures Myshuryn Rog.
3 October	Konev receives the 5th Guards Tank Army.
8–9 October	A German counter-attack against the Myshuryn Rog bridgehead fails.
12 October	Vatutin's first offensive to break out of the Bukrin bridgehead fails.
15 October	1.Panzerarmee is forced to evacuate the Zaporozhe bridgehead. Konev attacks with the 5th Guards Tank Army and achieves a breakthrough.

20 October	Stavka redesignates all of the fronts involved in the Lower Dnepr operation; Voronezh Front becomes 1st Ukrainian Front, Steppe Front becomes 2nd Ukrainian Front, South-Western Front becomes 3rd Ukrainian Front and Southern Front becomes 4th Ukrainian Front.
23 October	6.Armee abandons Melitopol.
25 October	1.Panzerarmee abandons Dnepropetrovsk; the 3rd Guards Tank Army begins to move from Bukrin to Lyutezh.
28 October	A German counter-attack is launched against the 5th Guards Tank Army near Krivoi Rog.
3 November	The 38th Army begins to break out from the Lyutezh bridgehead. Führer Directive 51 shifts priority of replacements to the Western Front.
5 November	The 3rd Guards Tank Army cuts the roads into Kiev and captures the rail junction at Fastov.
6 November	Kiev is liberated.
13 November	The 1st Guards Cavalry Corps (previously held in reserve) and 23rd Rifle Corps capture Zhitomir.
20 November	A German armoured counter-attack retakes Zhitomir.
23 November	German armoured pincers create a small pocket near Brusilov.
6–10 December	A German counter-attack is launched at Radomyschyl.
18 December	1.SS-Panzer-Division Leibstandarte SS Adolf Hitler (LSSAH) and 1.Panzer-Division attack near Meleni.
24 December	Vatutin's 1st Ukrainian Front begins a major offensive with the 1st Tank Army and 3rd Guards Tank Army against 4.Panzerarmee.
30 December	4.Panzerarmee abandons Korosten and Zhitomir.

1944

7 February	The Nikopol bridgehead is evacuated.

OPPOSING COMMANDERS

GERMAN

Generalfeldmarschall Erich von Manstein (1887–1973) had been commander of Heeresgruppe Süd since February 1943, and prior to that Heeresgruppe Don during the Stalingrad crisis. Von Manstein was the consummate general staff (*Grosser Generalstab*) officer and he had one of the best operational minds in the German Army (*Heer*), which was demonstrated by his role in developing the plan that demolished the French Army in 1940. As commander of 11.Armee in 1941–42, von Manstein conquered the Crimea and achieved one of the most lopsided victories of World War II in the Kerch Peninsula in May 1942. Taking command of Heeresgruppe Don in November 1942, von Manstein worked wonders in delaying the Soviet Winter Counter-Offensive and stabilised the southern front with his 'Backhand Blow' counter-offensive at Kharkov in February–March 1943. Von Manstein was a skilled practitioner of the art of manoeuvre warfare, but was not as well suited for defensive warfare. Furthermore, von Manstein had a tendency to underestimate the Red Army and did not appreciate that it was evolving into a much more capable force than the poorly led formations he had smashed so easily in 1941–42.

Generalfeldmarschall Erich von Manstein meets Hitler at Zaporozhe on 18 March 1943 just before the 'Backhand Blow' counter-offensive. Hitler had great confidence in von Manstein due to his success in conquering the Crimea and recapturing Kharkov, but changed his opinion when Heeresgruppe Süd continued to retreat and failed to stop the Red Army at the Dnepr. Eventually, Hitler came to regard von Manstein as a defeatist. (Author's collection)

Generaloberst Hermann Hoth (1885–1971) had been commander of 4.Panzerarmee since May 1942. Although he was an infantry officer, Hoth was one of the most experienced senior-level Panzer leaders in the *Heer*, having successfully led a motorised corps in Poland and France, then Panzergruppe 3 during Operation *Barbarossa* and 4.Panzerarmee during the Stalingrad campaign. Hoth also knew what it was to fail spectacularly: he had led the disastrous rescue mission to reach Stalingrad and then the failed offensive to reach Kursk. Like von Manstein, Hoth was trained in the general staff and had an appreciation for operational-level manoeuvre. As a commander, Hoth was an able planner and knew how to handle his troops well, but he was worn out by four years of non-stop campaigning and he was beginning to show signs of exhaustion.

Generaloberst Eberhard von Mackensen (1889–1969) was commander of 1.Panzerarmee from November 1942 to October 1943. Von Mackensen was the son of the famous August von Mackensen and a stereotypical Prussian cavalry officer. During Operation *Barbarossa*, he commanded III Armeekorps (mot.), which later became III Panzerkorps in the invasion of the Caucasus in 1942. Towards the end of the Caucasus campaign, von Mackensen took over 1.Panzerarmee when Generalfeldmarschall Ewald von Kleist moved up to take command of Heeresgruppe A. Von Mackensen was aggressive and a good team player, but did not get along well with Hitler. During the Dnepr campaign, von Mackensen was sent to Italy to command 14.Armee but he was relieved in July 1944 and saw no further service.

Generaloberst Hermann Hoth was exhausted by years of non-stop campaigning and his 4. Panzerarmee was roughly handled throughout the Dnepr campaign. Hitler blamed him for the loss of Kiev and eventually relieved him of command. (Bundesarchiv Bild 101I-218-0530-10; photo: Geller)

Generaloberst Hans-Valentin Hube (1890–1944) was made commander of 1. Panzerarmee on 29 October 1943. During World War I, Hube lost his left arm in France in 1914 but returned to the front in 1915 to command an infantry company. He was gassed in 1918. Hube remained in the post-war Reichswehr and served in a variety of infantry command and training slots during the inter-war period

Generaloberst Eberhard von Mackensen at the Dnepr Dam near Zaporozhe, after it had been repaired. The Red Army blew up the dam in 1941 in order to deny its hydroelectric power to the Germans, and Organisation Todt was not able to completely restore the dam until spring 1943. Hitler was extremely reluctant to abandon facilities with economic value, but the Germans were forced to blow up the Dnepr Dam when they abandoned the Zaporozhe bridgehead. (Author's collection)

and then the first campaigns of World War II. After the 1940 French campaign, Hube was selected to command the newly formed 16.Panzer-Division and he led this formation during Operation *Barbarossa* in 1941 and the subsequent Stalingrad campaign in 1942. Hube's division was the first German unit to reach the Volga and when his division was encircled in the Stalingrad pocket, Hitler ordered him flown out in December 1942 because he did not want to lose commanders of his calibre. Hube was a very tough, aggressive and experienced commander – the kind who could hold his troops together even in desperately adverse conditions.

General der Infanterie Otto Wöhler (1894–1987) had been commander of 8.Armee, formerly Armee-Abteilung Kempf, since 18 August 1943. Wöhler was a professional general staff officer who had served as von Manstein's chief of staff in 11.Armee between 1940 and 1942, then as chief of staff of Heeresgruppe Mitte in 1942–43. However, his only real command experience was four months with I Armeekorps in Heeresgruppe Nord's Volkhov sector between April and August 1943. Wöhler was selected to command because he was intelligent and followed von Manstein's orders, unlike his predecessor, but he took command of 8.Armee only weeks before it began retreating to the Dnepr.

General der Infanterie Otto Wöhler speaking with Generaloberst Ferdinand Schörner in 1944, when Schörner was in command of Heeresgruppe Südukraine. Note Schörner's Pour le Mérite medal, which he earned in World War I. Wöhler's hard-pressed 8.Armee had to pay the price in the Korsun pocket for Hitler's unwillingness to abandon the last German positions along the Dnepr. (Bundesarchiv Bild 183-2007-0313-500; photo: Heinz Mittelstaedt)

Generaloberst Karl-Adolf Hollidt (1891–1985) had been commander of 6.Armee, formerly Armee-Abteilung Hollidt, since November 1942. Hollidt served as a junior infantry officer in World War I, rising to command a battalion on the Eastern Front. During the inter-war period he received general-staff training, which allowed him to alternate between command and staff assignments. He commanded an infantry division in 1941 and then XXVII Armeekorps in 1942. By chance, after the Soviet encirclement of 6.Armee at Stalingrad, Hollidt was picked to lead a scratch force that held the new German front west of the Don River. Hollidt proved to be an excellent commander in adversity, able to conduct a well-organised delaying action or retreat.

SOVIET

General Nikolai Vatutin (1901–44) had been commander of the Voronezh Front (later redesignated 1st Ukrainian Front) since March 1943. Unlike his opponents, Vatutin came from a humble peasant background and worked his way upward in the Red Army by a combination of skill as a planner and currying political favour. He spent the (unusually long) period 1926–34 as a student at the Frunze Military Academy in Moscow, then graduated from the General Staff (*General'nogo shtaba*) Academy in 1937. Vatutin was noticed by Zhukov and served as his chief of staff in the Kiev Military District from 1938 to 1940. At the start of World War II, Vatutin was chief of staff of the North-Western Front and he organised the counter-attack at Soltsy in July 1941 that mauled one of von Manstein's divisions. Thereafter, Vatutin served as a Stavka representative at Stalingrad and then took command of the South-Western Front during the Soviet 1942/43 Winter Counter-Offensive. He made one serious mistake, which was misinterpreting von Manstein's intentions in February 1943. Vatutin believed that Heeresgruppe Süd was withdrawing to the Dnepr when in fact it was preparing a major counter-stroke, which resulted in the defeat of Vatutin's forces. Nevertheless, Vatutin learned from this defeat and he proved to be one of the most capable and adaptable of any of the Red Army's front-level commanders.

General-polkovnik Ivan Konev (1897–1973) had been commander of the Steppe Front (later redesignated 2nd Ukrainian Front) since July 1943. Konev also came from a peasant background, was a graduate of the Frunze and was not afraid to use political connections to assist his career. However, unlike Vatutin, Konev had considerably more command experience, both in the inter-war period and during the early stages of the Russo-German War. Konev was given command of the Kalinin Front in October 1941 and made a name for himself during the defence of Moscow. However, his command of the Western Front and then the North-Western Front in 1942–43 earned him little renown due to the static, attritional nature of combat on these fronts. Konev was a ruthless political animal and very jealous of the success of others, particularly Vatutin and Zhukov.

General Georgy Zhukov (left) conferring with General Nikolai Vatutin (right) and his chief of staff General-leytenant Aleksandr N. Bogoliubov. Zhukov's role as a Stavka representative was to coordinate the actions of multi-front operations like the Lower Dnepr offensive and to ensure that front-level planning was in line with Stavka's strategic intent. However, Vatutin was in command of the 1st Ukrainian Front and he and his staff were primarily responsible for the liberation of Kiev, not Zhukov. (Courtesy of the Central Museum of the Armed Forces, Moscow via Stavka)

General Rodion Malinovsky (1898–1967) had been commander of the South-Western Front (later redesignated 3rd Ukrainian Front) since March 1943. Malinovsky grew up in abject poverty near Odessa. During World War I, he served in the Russian infantry brigade sent to France and remained there until 1918. Returning to Russia, he joined the Red Army and was educated at the Frunze Military Academy from 1927 to 1930. In 1936, Malinovsky went to Spain for two years as an advisor to the Republicans. Despite suspicions about his foreign contacts, Malinovsky managed to survive Stalin's purges and was commanding a rifle corps near Odessa at the start of World War II. He rose steadily to army, then front-level command by the end of 1941. He fought in the Caucasus in 1942; then, as commander of the 2nd Guards Army, he stopped Hoth's effort to reach the trapped 6.Armee at Stalingrad. Malinovsky was a tough, competent commander.

General Rodion Malinovsky, commander of the 3rd Ukrainian Front. Malinovsky was a dependable, if unexceptional, commander who underperformed during the Dnepr campaign. (Author's collection)

General Fyodor I. Tolbukhin (1894–1949) had been commander of the Southern Front (later redesignated 4th Ukrainian Front) since March 1943. Tolbukhin served as a junior officer in the Tsarist army during World War I, then switched to the Red Army in 1918. He spent most of the inter-war period and early period of World War II as a professional staff officer, usually in secondary areas such as the Transcaucasus and the Crimea. In July 1942 Tolbukhin was given command of the 58th Army, which he led ably during the battle of Stalingrad. Tolbukhin was a set-piece type of commander, inclined to conduct operations by the book.

General Fyodor I. Tolbukhin, commander of the 4th Ukrainian Front. Tolbukhin had a complicated mission, being responsible for crossing the Dnepr at Zaporozhe and liberating the Crimea. (Author's collection)

General Konstantin K. Rokossovsky confers with Vatutin. Rokossovsky was one of the Red Army's best front-level commanders and known for careful staff work. By late 1943, the Red Army had a cadre of skilled operational commanders like Vatutin and Rokossovsky who were capable of out-fighting their German opponents. The days of inept front-line leadership ruining Red Army offensive operations with a string of bad decisions were over. (Courtesy of the Central Museum of the Armed Forces, Moscow via Stavka)

General-leytenant Pavel Rotmistrov, commander of the 5th Guards Tank Army, in a forward observation post with General-polkovnik Ivan Konev. Despite his school-teacher looks, Rotmistrov was a capable tank leader and he led the breakout from the Myshuryn Rog bridgehead in October 1943. Konev was one of Zhukov's main competitors, and was equally brutal and politically cunning. (Courtesy of the Central Museum of the Armed Forces, Moscow via Stavka)

General-polkovnik Pavel S. Rybalko (1892–1948) had been commander of the 3rd Guards Tank Army since September 1942. Rybalko was born near Kharkov and joined the Red cavalry during the Russian Civil War. In the 1930s, he switched to mechanised forces, but spent the next five years in training assignments in Moscow and Kazan, not with actual tank units. At the start of World War II, Rybalko was an instructor at the Tank School in Kazan and to his chagrin he remained there until May 1942. At this point, Rybalko was sent to the front as deputy commander of the newly formed 3rd Tank Army; five months later he took command of this formation. Rybalko was a highly unorthodox Soviet commander in that he was both an academic interested in learning higher-level manoeuvre warfare doctrine, and also someone who enjoyed getting on tanks and learning how to operate them. He was a very 'hands on' and 'up front' type of commander, which was unusual for the Red Army, where most commanders rarely made an effort to directly interact with front-line troops. Although badly defeated by von Manstein's 'Backhand Blow' counter-offensive at Kharkov in March 1943, Rybalko learned from that defeat and was on the way to becoming one of the best armoured commanders in the Red Army.

OPPOSING FORCES

GERMAN

Armour

By mid-September 1943, the eight Panzer divisions and three elite Panzergrenadier divisions within Heeresgruppe Süd were all severely depleted after two months of heavy combat. These Panzer divisions were no longer the proud, strong formations that had been laboriously rebuilt during the spring of 1943, but battered units that were forced to borrow horses from the infantry to make up for their insufficient numbers of trucks. Furthermore, the Germans only had 700 operational tanks and 400 assault guns left on the entire Eastern Front – less than one-third of what they had at the start of July. (The total strength on 10 September 1943 was 1,748 tanks and 997 assault guns, with an operational readiness rate of 40 per cent.) Hundreds of tanks were in repair shops and when the retreat began, most would be abandoned or blown up. Von Manstein's emaciated Panzer divisions averaged no more than 10–30 operational tanks each – usually a mix of PzKpfw III and PzKpfw IV medium tanks – and about half their complement of Panzergrenadiers. The strongest armoured unit, SS-Panzergrenadier-Division 'Totenkopf', had 31 tanks and 15 assault guns still operational. Although a few battalions of the new PzKpfw V Panther tank arrived during the course of the Dnepr campaign, at the start only the 'Das Reich', 'Totenkopf' and 'Grossdeutschland' divisions had any Panthers and very few were operational. Due to the inability of German industry to replace losses of tanks, trucks and other equipment, the Panzer divisions were now permanently handicapped. Increasingly, *Panzer-Kampfgruppen* (armoured battle groups) included unusual attachments, such as replacement battalions or security police, to serve as ad hoc infantry support.

Given the paucity of tanks, the most useful units for a mobile delay operation like the Dnepr campaign were the Panzer division's organic Panzer-Aufklärungs-Abteilung, which was authorised a total of 122 half-tracks and 18 armoured cars; these reconnaissance battalions had the mobility and the firepower to respond quickly to unexpected enemy advances. Heeresgruppe Süd also had nine *Sturmgeschütz-Abteilungen* (assault gun battalions) available with the excellent StuG III, as well as a few self-propelled *Panzerjäger-Abteilungen* equipped with a mix of Marder, Ferdinand and Hornisse tank destroyers. During the Dnepr campaign, von Manstein did receive strong armoured reinforcements, including five refitted Panzer

A tracked Maultier vehicle delivering ammunition, December 1943. Some of the elite units had improved logistic vehicles like this, but even the Panzer divisions were becoming dependent upon horses and carts to deliver supplies. (Bundesarchiv, Bild 101I-709-0322-16; photo: Gerhard Gronefeld)

divisions and two *schwere Panzer-Abteilungen* (heavy tank battalions) equipped with Tiger I tanks, but they did not arrive until the Soviets were already across the Dnepr in strength.

While veteran German tankers still maintained a significant tactical edge over Soviet tankers, the Panzer divisions were much reduced in operational effectiveness because of the general decline of the German combined-arms team. Without adequate air, artillery or infantry support, the Panzer divisions were no longer capable of achieving decisive results. Although von Manstein hoped to mass his armour to conduct operational-level counter-strokes as he had in the past, Germany's limited resources forced him to modify his tactics. Instead of keeping Panzer divisions in the rear until ready to attack, the lack of infantry to maintain an adequate *Hauptkampflinie* (HKL – main line of resistance) forced von Manstein to use armour in the forward lines to hold their own sectors of the front. Instead of using armour en masse, the Germans were increasingly forced to employ a zone defence, with decentralised operations and armour used in local counter-attacks to contain enemy breakthroughs. Limited fuel reserves also severely impacted German armoured mobility by late 1943, particularly for the fuel-hungry Panther and Tiger tanks.

Infantry

Even before the retreat to the Dnepr began, many of the infantry divisions in Heeresgruppe Süd were reduced by combat losses into brigade- or regimental-size *Kampfgruppen*. In the hard-hit 8.Armee, for example, eight of its 12 infantry divisions were reduced to 30–50 per cent of their *Kampfstärke* (fighting strength) by the beginning of September.[1] Only a handful of divisions, recently transferred from other fronts, were still fully combat effective. Once the retreat began, the horse-drawn artillery and support units in the infantry divisions were unable to stay ahead of pursuing Soviet armoured units and were highly vulnerable to air attack. A great deal of horses, trucks, artillery and other equipment was lost in the retreat to the Dnepr, which greatly reduced the defensive capabilities of Heeresgruppe

1   *Kampfstärke* included the available infantry, as well as Panzerjäger, combat engineers, reconnaissance troops, fusiliers and any attached combat troops. For a German infantry division in mid-1943, a nominal *Kampfstärke* was in the region of 4,000 troops.

Süd's remaining infantry. It was the severe lack of infantry which most hampered von Manstein's ability to hold the Dnepr and the use of security troops in the front line was a mark of desperation.

German intelligence

The relative ability of the OKH to determine Soviet intentions and objectives shaped the campaign. Initially, the OKH made a fair assessment of where the Soviets would attempt to cross the Dnepr, but once the battle for the bridgeheads began in earnest, the Germans were unable to discern the Soviet main effort. By late September, there were so many Soviet bridgeheads over the Dnepr that the OKH could not determine which sectors were the most important, so von Manstein had to spread his limited resources across a wide front. Later, the Soviet use of *maskirovka* (deception) managed to conceal the redeployment of Rybalko's 3rd Guards Tank Army from the Bukrin to the Lyutezh bridgehead, which caught von Manstein completely off balance. Nor were the Germans able to detect the massive reinforcement of Vatutin's 1st Ukrainian Front in December. Without adequate aerial reconnaissance, German intelligence was unable to predict where the next blow would fall and consequently, von Manstein was unable to parry the enemy's attacks.

Luftwaffe

For the first time in clear-weather months, von Manstein had to conduct a campaign without adequate support from the Luftwaffe. Luftflotte 4 still had about 600 combat aircraft, but only half were operational; most of its constituent formations had been badly depleted by two months of non-stop air action and several air groups had already been sent to refit in Germany. At the start of the Dnepr campaign, Luftflotte 4 had six *Jagdgruppen* with a total of about 170 fighters (108 Fw 190A and 62 Bf 109G), mostly based at Poltava. In order to cover the Dnepr River crossing sites, II./Jagdgeschwader 54 was relocated to Kiev before the retreat began; it had 22 Fw 190A fighters. Since *Zitadelle* in July, II./Jagdgeschwader 54 had lost 85 fighters but received only 15 replacements. The VIII Fliegerkorps still had some close air support

A flight of three He-111 bombers over the Ukraine, 1943. For the first time, Luftwaffe support to Heeresgruppe Süd proved insufficient. Despite repeated attempts to bomb Soviet pontoon bridges over the Dnepr, the Luftwaffe failed to sever the Red Army's lines of communications across the river. (Bundesarchiv Bild 101I-641-4548-24; photo: W. Wanderer)

capability with about 160 Ju 87D Stukas from Sturzkampfgeschwader 2 and Sturzkampfgeschwader 77, which quickly relocated behind the Dnepr, but without fighter cover the Stukas were very vulnerable. Luftflotte 4 also had eight bomber groups with a total of 270 He 111 and Ju 88 medium bombers, mostly based at Kirovograd. Badly outnumbered, with limited fuel and replacements, the Luftwaffe in Russia could now only occasionally influence local operations.

SOVIET

Tank armies

In 1942, the Red Army had thought that grouping a large number of tanks into an army-size formation would be adequate to conduct operational manoeuvre warfare. However, it quickly came to realise that without supporting arms, armour could not succeed on its own. The new tank armies of 1943 usually consisted of two tank corps and one mechanised corps, with a nominal authorised strength of about 500 tanks. However, like the German Panzer divisions, the Soviet tank armies were depleted after months of heavy combat and were unable to field more than 250–300 tanks each. Yet Soviet industry was able to replace losses fairly rapidly and the Red Army could restore even a badly depleted tank army in just one month. New mobile tank workshops followed the tank armies and repaired hundreds of knocked-out tanks. Furthermore, the Red Army was phasing out most of their light tanks in favour of a new tank brigade structure consisting entirely of medium tanks, either domestic T-34/76 models or Lend-Lease M4A2 Shermans or Valentines. While the T-34/76 Model 1943 was outmatched by the occasional Tiger I or Panther, it could hold its own against the other German medium tanks and enjoyed a large numerical superiority.

The SU-76 self-propelled gun had first entered service in January 1943 but the initial version had a number of mechanical defects. It was not until the summer of 1943 that the improved SU-76M began to enter service and although it still had faults, this weapon provided Soviet mechanised units with their first effective mobile fire support. The SU-76M was particularly useful in reducing German strongpoints and in city fighting. (Courtesy of the Central Museum of the Armed Forces, Moscow via Stavka)

In addition, the Soviet tank armies were evolving into balanced combined-arms formations and now included anti-tank units, engineers and self-propelled guns (SU-76M or SU-122). The one remaining serious deficiency was a reliance on BM-13 multiple rocket launchers and 120mm mortars for mobile fire support, instead of tube artillery. Consequently, tank armies could not be used effectively in the breakthrough role. Rather, Red Army senior leaders believed that tank armies were intended for the exploitation role in loose accordance with the pre-war Deep Battle doctrine and not before combined-arms armies had achieved a breakthrough. The tank army itself was intended as a mobile group (*podvizhnyi grupp*) for the front commander and within the tank army, a reinforced tank brigade was designated as the advance guard. Built upon the dependable T-34/76 medium tank, Soviet tank armies were capable of conducting very rapid operational movements of up to 400km within 72 hours. Although the number of tactical radios in Soviet tank units tripled during 1943, the limited number of long-range radios at brigade and corps level made command control problematic and pursuit operations often resulted in the constituent corps becoming too spread out to coordinate.

Combined-arms armies

By mid-1943 the Red Army was employing combined-arms armies (*obshchevoyskovykh armiy*) that were built upon two–three rifle corps, each with two–three rifle divisions. At full strength, corps-level support usually included a tank brigade with 40–50 tanks or a regiment of 20–25 SU-76M self-propelled guns. In theory, the rifle corps could have up to 28,000 troops, but in reality most Soviet rifle units operated at 50–60 per cent strength, so a typical rifle corps in late 1943 might field 7,000–8,000 infantry. As the Red Army advanced across the Ukraine, local civilians were drafted into units to replace losses; these recruits received little training but they helped rifle corps to continue operations despite horrific casualties. Surprisingly, there was no shortage of trained junior infantry officers in the Red Army after mid-1943 due to a massive training effort in 1942–43. The better-quality combined-arms armies, comprising guards and airborne units, were capable of independent offensive operations and were typically used to create a breakthrough for armoured units to exploit.

The Red Army's ability to mass heavy artillery against targets proved highly lethal to German infantry field works by 1943–44. The Artillery Corps also began to receive new weapons after the battle of Kursk, such as the 152mm howitzer M1943 or D-1, which entered service in late 1943. (Courtesy of the Central Museum of the Armed Forces, Moscow via Stavka)

Artillery

The Red Army formed its first artillery divisions in October 1942 and its first artillery corps in April 1943. Vatutin's Voronezh Front was provided with the 7th Artillery Corps, comprising two artillery divisions and a Guards Mortar (rocket) division; the corps comprised over

A Soviet 76.2mm field gun towed by a US-built cargo truck. By mid-1943, Lend-Lease was supplying a large percentage of the Red Army's trucks and other wheeled vehicles, since Soviet industry was focused on tanks and artillery. The Red Army's advance to the Dnepr and exploitation across it would have been greatly slowed without the availability of Lend-Lease support vehicles. (Nik Cornish at www.Stavka.org.uk)

25,000 troops, 960 guns, mortars and rocket launchers and 4,500 trucks. This firepower included 24 203mm and 64 152mm howitzers and 216 BM-30 (300mm) multiple rocket launchers. Rather than just an accumulation of artillery pieces, the Artillery Corps represented a pool of trained artillerymen who knew how to properly plan, coordinate and execute complex fire-support missions. The creation of the Artillery Corps represented a major step towards professionalism in the Red Army and gave Soviet offensives an important combat multiplier. Instead of the poorly planned and executed fire support of 1941–42, the Red Army of mid-1943 had learned how to mass its artillery to pulverise German front-line divisions and create the conditions for a successful breakthrough.

Airborne

Stavka was eager to employ its airborne forces to assist an assault crossing of the Dnepr and had plenty of trained paratroopers available. At the start of the Lower Dnepr offensive, Vatutin was provided with a provisional airborne corps consisting of 10,000 paratroopers from the 1st, 3rd and 5th Guards Airborne brigades. These were good units, with plenty of organic firepower. However, the Red Army had very limited experience in planning large-scale airborne operations and the lack of a permanent airborne staff left the airborne units at the mercy of front-level staff who did not put a high priority on their needs. Furthermore, the *Voyenno-Vozdushnye Sily* (VVS – Military Air Forces) did not have a large amount of air transports available and in September 1943 only 48 Li-2 transports, a licensed-built copy of the American DC-3, were available for the Dnepr operation. Some bombers were also pressed into service and a few gliders, but the VVS could barely deliver 1,000 paratroops in a single lift. Even worse, the navigation capabilities of the VVS transport units at night were so poor that the probability of a concentrated airdrop on a specific landing zone was next to zero.

Engineers

Most of the Red Army's pre-war pontoon engineer units were lost during the hectic retreats of the summer of 1941 and it was not until November 1942 that the NKO (*Narodny Kommissariat Oborony* – People's Commissariat of

Defence) decided to begin re-forming engineer bridging units. In order to conduct mobile offensive operations, the Red Army was going to need the ability to quickly bridge rivers in order to push tanks and artillery across. By late 1943, the Red Army had four types of bridging units: a 2,000-man pontoon brigade (*Pontonno-mostovyye brigady*) with four battalions equipped with the N2P and DMP-42 pontoon bridge kits, a 900-man pontoon regiment (*Pontonno-mostovyye polka*) with the same equipment but only two battalions, a 450-man independent pontoon battalion (*Otdel'nyye pontonno-mostovyye batal'ony* or *opomb*) and a heavy pontoon regiment equipped with the TMP pontoon bridge. A motorised pontoon battalion relied upon 86 ZIS-5 trucks to move its bridging equipment, but the non-motorised pontoon battalions had no trucks attached and depended upon front-level assets for transportation.

Table 1: Soviet bridging assets

Name	Length (m)	Weight capacity (tons)	Time to construct
N2P	160	60	3 hours
DMP-42	620	50	3–4 hours
TMP	450	100	3–5 hours

Soviet tactical bridging was far more advanced than that possessed by the Germans. With the standard N2P kit, Soviet engineers could construct a 35t-capacity bridge across a 106m-wide gap in less than four hours or assemble pontoons into motorised ferries. However, for bridging a river as wide as the Dnepr, the Red Army relied upon the TMP bridge, which could be used in tandem to cross wider gaps. At the start of the Lower Dnepr Offensive, the four Soviet fronts involved had a total of five pontoon brigades, two pontoon regiments and eight separate pontoon battalions. However, the bulk of the bridging assets were in the South-Western and Southern fronts, while Vatutin had only a single pontoon brigade and Konev had none at all.

Logistics

Operational-level logistics was not a strong suit in the Red Army, but in order to sustain protracted, multi-front offensives, in June 1943 the NKO began to reform and streamline its rear services in order to provide fronts with the ability to move large quantities of fuel, ammunition and replacements to forward units during an offensive. The Red Army utilised a 'push' system of logistics, with supplies sent from depots in the rear to army-level depots, rather than the 'pull' system used by the Germans. In addition to transport shortfalls, ammunition and fuel stockpiles at the front were very low after weeks of heavy combat and this impaired the ability of the Red

Soviet scouts use a tactical radio to send spot reports to their battalion headquarters. Although the Red Army had been very deficient in terms of tactical communications in 1941 and 1942, with most radios only at the regiment level and above, by late 1943 more and better radios were provided to lower-echelon units. While communications security remained a sore spot, improved Soviet tactical communications played an important role in raising the Red Army's performance on the battlefield. (Courtesy of the Central Museum of the Armed Forces, Moscow via Stavka)

Army to conduct high-tempo mobile operations for more than a few days. Unlike the Germans, the Soviets lacked the air transport fleet to conduct large-scale aerial resupply and due to the poor road network, logistics relied very heavily upon the rail network. However, the German 'scorched earth' tactics employed during the retreat to the Dnepr damaged much of the rail network, so it was imperative for the Red Army to repair rail lines as rapidly as possible. Each front received a 3,000-man Railway Repair Brigade, which was also capable of reconstructing bridges.

However, during a mobile operation like the Lower Dnepr campaign, the Red Army relied primarily upon motor transport to push supplies forward. Each front was provided with a truck brigade with three–six battalions of trucks and each army received one–three truck battalions. A truck battalion typically had 100 trucks, either Soviet-built GAZ-AA (1.5t) or ZIS-5 (3t) trucks or American-built Studebaker or CCKW 2.5t trucks. Thus, a front with four armies might have 1,000–1,500 trucks (with roughly 20 per cent in repair), with an approximate lift capacity of 2,000–3,000t. Army and Front-level transport units focused on moving fuel, ammunition and spare parts forward, while the supply of rations and fodder was delegated to the small logistical support elements in each rifle division (roughly 60 trucks and 250 horse-drawn wagons with a cargo capacity of about 200–250t). However, since a typical Soviet combined-arms army had a daily supply requirement of about 3,000t, including 1,600t of ammunition, 550t of fuel and 1,000t of rations/fodder, there was a significant shortfall between demand and cargo capacity when the distance to railheads exceeded 100km or more. Consequently, Soviet combat units tended to live hand-to-mouth during mobile operations and forward stockpiling levels of fuel and ammunition were minimal. Soviet troops were poorly fed and half their nutritional needs were met by Lend-Lease canned-food goods. After mid-1943, the arrival of large numbers of Lend-Lease all-wheel drive trucks did ease Soviet logistical problems significantly, but lingering shortfalls inhibited the speed of Soviet offensives until 1945.

The Red Army of late 1943 was very different from the formations employed a year earlier, which still had ill-equipped troops sent into battle. During the Lower Dnepr campaign, Soviet infantry was better equipped and even had tactical field telephones in use. The Red Army's junior leadership was also much improved, as a cadre of experienced veterans was now at the front. (Author's collection)

ORDER OF BATTLE, 20 SEPTEMBER 1943

GERMAN

HEERESGRUPPE MITTE (GENERALFELDMARSCHALL GÜNTHER VON KLUGE)

2.Armee (General der Infanterie Walter Weiss)
XX Armeekorps (General der Artillerie Rudolf Freiherr von Roman)
  45.Infanterie-Division
  86.Infanterie-Division

  137.Infanterie-Division
LVI Panzerkorps (General der Infanterie Friedrich Hossbach)
  4.Panzer-Division (Generalleutnant Dietrich von Saucken)
  12.Panzer-Division (Generalleutnant Erpo Freiherr von Bodenhausen)
  5.Panzer-Division (Oberst Karl Decker) – en route from 9.Armee

HEERESGRUPPE SÜD (GENERALFELDMARSCHALL ERICH VON MANSTEIN)

4.Panzerarmee (Generaloberst Hermann Hoth)

VII Armeekorps (General der Artillerie Ernst-Eberhard Hell)
  68.Infanterie-Division
  75.Infanterie-Division
  88.Infanterie-Division
  Kampfgruppen from 82.Infanterie and 327.Infanterie divisions
  Sturmgeschütz-Abteilung 208
XIII Armeekorps (Generalleutnant Arthur Hauffe)
  327.Infanterie-Division
  340.Infanterie-Division
  213.Sicherungs-Division
  Kampfgruppen from 183.Infanterie and 208.Infanterie divisions
 LIX Armeekorps (General der Infanterie Kurt von der Chevallerie)
  8.Panzer-Division (Generalmajor Gottfried Frölich)
  Kampfgruppe 2.Panzer-Division
  217.Infanterie-Division
XXIV Panzerkorps (General der Panzertruppen Walther Nehring)
  10.Panzergrenadier-Division (Generalleutnant August Schmidt)
  Kampfgruppen from 34.Infanterie, 57.Infanterie, 112.Infanterie and 255.Infanterie divisions
XXXXVIII Panzerkorps (General der Panzertruppe Otto von Knobelsdorff)
  19.Panzer-Division (Oberst Hans Källner)

8.Armee (General der Infanterie Otto Wöhler)

III Panzerkorps (General der Panzertruppe Hermann Breith)
  6.Panzer-Division (Oberst Rudolf Freiherr von Waldenfels)
  7.Panzer-Division (Generalmajor Hasso von Manteuffel)
  SS-Panzergrenadier-Division 'Wiking' (SS-Brigadeführer Herbert Otto Gille)
  Panzergrenadier-Division 'Grossdeutschland' (Generalleutnant Walter Hörnlein)
XXXXVII Panzerkorps (General der Panzertruppe Joachim Lemelsen)
  3.Panzer-Division (Generalleutnant Franz Westhoven)
  SS-Panzergrenadier-Division 'Das Reich' (SS-Gruppenführer Walter Krüger)
  SS-Panzergrenadier-Division 'Totenkopf' (SS-Brigadeführer Hermann Priess)
XI Armeekorps (General der Panzertruppe Erhard Raus)
  Kampfgruppen from 106.Infanterie, 167.Infanterie and 168. Infanterie divisions
  198.Infanterie-Division
  320.Infanterie-Division
  schwere Panzer-Abteilung 503
  Sturmgeschütz-Abteilung 905
Under 8.Armee control:
  72.Infanterie-Division

1.Panzerarmee (Generaloberst Eberhard von Mackensen)

XXX Armeekorps (General der Artillerie Maximilian Fretter-Pico)
  125.Infanterie-Division
  257.Infanterie-Division
  387.Infanterie-Division
  Kampfgruppe from 38.Infanterie-Division
  Kampfgruppe from 62.Infanterie-Division
XXXX Panzerkorps (Generaloberst Gotthard Heinrici)
  23.Panzer-Division (Generalleutnant Nikolaus von Vormann)
  16.Panzergrenadier-Division (Generalleutnant Gerhard Graf von Schwerin)
  304.Infanterie-Division
  323.Infanterie-Division
  Kampfgruppe from 306.Infanterie-Division
  Kampfgruppe from 335.Infanterie-Division
  schwere Panzer-Abteilung 506
LVII Panzerkorps (General der Panzertruppe Friedrich Kirchner)
  15.Infanterie-Division
  46.Infanterie-Division
  257.Infanterie-Division
  SS-Kavallerie-Division
  Sturmgeschütz-Abteilung 203 and 232
XVII Armeekorps
  294.Infanterie-Division
  333.Infanterie-Division
LII Armeekorps (General der Infanterie Eugen Ott)
  355.Infanterie-Division
  Kampfgruppe from 161.Infanterie-Division
  Kampfgruppe from 293.Infanterie-Division
  Sturmgeschütz-Abteilung 228 and 261
Under 1.Panzerarmee control:
  Sturmgeschütz-Abteilung 236

HEERESGRUPPE A (GENERALFELDMARSCHALL EWALD VON KLEIST)

6.Armee (Generaloberst Karl-Adolf Hollidt)

IV Armeekorps (General der Infanterie Friedrich Mieth)
  17.Panzer-Division (Generalmajor Karl-Friedrich von der Meden)
  3.Gebirgs-Division
  101.Jäger-Division
  302.Infanterie-Division
  5.Luftwaffen-Feld-Division
  Sturmgeschütz-Abteilung 259
XXIX Armeekorps (General der Artillerie Erich Brandenberger)
  9.Panzer-Division (Oberst Erwin Jollasse)
  13.Panzer-Division (Oberst Eduard Hauser)
  17.Infanterie-Division
  111.Infanterie-Division
  Kampfgruppe from 336.Infanterie-Division
  15.Luftwaffen-Feld-Division
  Kavallerie-Regiment Süd
  Romanian 24th Infantry Division
  Sturmgeschütz-Abteilung 243

Luftflotte 4 (Generaloberst Otto Dessloch)

I Fliegerkorps (Generalleutnant Karl Angerstein)

   Stab, I., II. and III./Jagdgeschwader 52 (Bf 109G)

   Stab, I. and II./Kampfgeschwader 3 (Ju 88)

   Stab, II. and III./Kampfgeschwader 27 (He 111)

   Stab, I. and III./Sturzkampfgeschwader 2 (Ju 87D)

IV Fliegerkorps (General Rudolf Meister)

   II./Kampfgeschwader 4 (He 111H)

   Stab, II./Kampfgeschwader 51 (Ju 88)

   Stab, I., II. and III./Kampfgeschwader 55 (He 111)

VIII Fliegerkorps (General der Flieger Hans Seidemann)

   I. and III./Jagdgeschwader 51 (Fw 190), IV./Jagdgeschwader 51 (Bf 109G)

   I. and II./Jagdgeschwader 54 (Fw 190)

   Stab, I., II. and III./Sturzkampfgeschwader 77 (Ju 87D)

   Stab, II./Schlachtgeschwader 1 (Fw 190A)

SOVIET

CENTRAL FRONT (GENERAL KONSTANTIN K. ROKOSSOVSKY)

13th Army (General-leytenant Nikolai P. Pukhov)

15th Rifle Corps (General-major Ivan I. Liudnikov)

   8th Rifle Division

   74th Rifle Division

   148th Rifle Division

28th Rifle Corps (General-major Aleksandr N. Nechaev)

   181st Rifle Division

   202nd Rifle Division

   211st Rifle Division

129th Tank Brigade

60th Army (General-leytenant Ivan D. Cherniakhovsky)

17th Guards Rifle Corps (General-leytenant Andrei L. Bondarev)

   6th Guards Rifle Division

   70th Guards Rifle Division

   75th Guards Rifle Division

18th Guards Rifle Corps (General-major Ivan M. Afonin)

   2nd Guards Airborne Division

   3rd Guards Airborne Division

   4th Guards Airborne Division

24th Rifle Corps (General-major Nikolai I. Kiriukhin)

   112th Rifle Division

   226th Rifle Division

   322nd Rifle Division

30th Rifle Corps (General-major Grigori S. Lazko)

   121st Rifle Division

   141st Rifle Division

   280th Rifle Division

77th Rifle Corps (General-major Petr M. Kozlov)

   132nd Rifle Division

   143rd Rifle Division

   280th Rifle Division

150th Tank Brigade

61st Army (General-leytenant Pavel A. Belov)

9th Guards Rifle Corps (General-major Arkady A. Boreiko)

   12th Guards Rifle Division

   76th Guards Rifle Division

   77th Guards Rifle Division

29th Rifle Corps (General-major Afanasii N. Slyshkin)

   15th Rifle Division

   55th Rifle Division

   81st Rifle Division

89th Rifle Corps (General-major Grigorii A. Khaliuzin)

   336th Rifle Division

   356th Rifle Division

   415th Rifle Division

68th Tank Brigade

2nd Tank Army (General-leytenant Semyon Bogdanov)

3rd Tank Corps (General-major Maksim D. Sinenko)

16th Tank Corps (General-major Vasily E. Grigoriev)

7th Guards Mechanised Corps (General-leytenant Ivan P. Korchagin)

11th Guards Tank Brigade

16th Air Army (General-leytenant Sergei I. Rudenko)

6th Fighter Aviation Corps

3rd Bomber Aviation Corps

6th Composite Aviation Corps

1st Guards Fighter Aviation Division

283rd Fighter Aviation Division

286th Fighter Aviation Division

2nd Guards Ground Attack Aviation Division

299th Ground Attack Aviation Division

VORONEZH FRONT (GENERAL NIKOLAI VATUTIN)

3rd Guards Tank Army (General-polkovnik Pavel S. Rybalko)

6th Guards Tank Corps (General-major Mitrofan I. Zink'kovich)

7th Guards Tank Corps (General-major Kirill P. Suleykov)

9th Mechanised Corps (General-major Konstantin A. Malygin)

91st Tank Brigade

4th Guards Army (General-leytenant Aleksei I. Zygin, KIA 27.09.43; General-leytenant Ivan V. Galanin)

20th Guards Rifle Corps (General-major Nikolai I. Biriukov)

   5th Guards Airborne Division

   7th Guards Airborne Division

   8th Guards Airborne Division

21st Guards Rifle Corps (General-major Petr I. Fomenko)

   68th Guards Rifle Division

   69th Guards Rifle Division

   80th Guards Rifle Division

3rd Guards Tank Corps (General-major Ivan A. Vovchenko)

5th Guards Army (General-leytenant Aleksei S. Zhadov); to Steppe Front by 01.10.43

32nd Guards Rifle Corps (General-major Aleksandr I. Rodimtsev)

   13th Guards Rifle Division

   95th Guards Rifle Division

   97th Guards Rifle Division

33rd Guards Rifle Corps
   6th Guards Airborne Division
   42nd Guards Rifle Division
   66th Guards Rifle Division
6th Guards Army (General-leytenant Ivan M. Chistiakov)
22nd Guards Rifle Corps (General-major Nikolai B. Ibianskii)
   67th Guards Rifle Division
   71st Guards Rifle Division
   163rd Rifle Division
23rd Guards Rifle Corps (General-major Nikolai T. Tavartkiladze)
   51st Guards Rifle Division
   52nd Guards Rifle Division
   90th Guards Rifle Division
5th Guards Tank Corps (General-leytenant Andrei G. Kravchenko)
20th Pontoon Battalion
1st Tank Army (General-leytenant Mikhail E. Katukov)
6th Tank Corps (General-leytenant Andrei L. Getman);
   redesignated 11th Guards Tank Corps 23.10.43
31st Tank Corps (Polkovnik Petr K. Zhidkov)
3rd Mechanised Corps (General-leytenant Semyon M. Krivoshein)
27th Army (General-leytenant Sergei G. Trofimenko)
71st Rifle Division
100th Rifle Division
147th Rifle Division
155th Rifle Division
166th Rifle Division
241st Rifle Division
17th Artillery Division
93rd Tank Brigade
38th Army (General-major Nikandr E. Chibisov; replaced by General-polkovnik Kirill S. Moskalenko 27.10.43)
50th Rifle Corps (General-major Sarkis S. Martirosian)
   232nd Rifle Division
   340th Rifle Division
51st Rifle Corps (General-major Petr P. Avdeenko)
   167th Rifle Division
   180th Rifle Division
   240th Rifle Division
108th Pontoon Battalion
40th Army (General-polkovnik Kirill S. Moskalenko; General-major Filipp F. Zhmachenko from 27.10.43)
47th Rifle Corps (General-major Serafim P. Merkulov)
   29th Rifle Division
   38th Rifle Division
   61st Rifle Division
   253rd Rifle Division
52nd Rifle Corps (General-major Frants I. Perkhorovich)
   237th Rifle Division
   309th Rifle Division
8th Guards Tank Corps (General-leytenant Aleksei F. Popov)
47th Army (General-major Filipp F. Zhmachenko – to 40th Army 27.10.43; General-leytenant Vitaliy S. Polenov)

21st Rifle Corps (General-major Vasily L. Abramov)
   206th Rifle Division
   218th Rifle Division
23rd Rifle Corps (General-major Nikita E. Chuvakov)
   23rd Rifle Division
   30th Rifle Division
   337th Rifle Division
3rd Guards Mechanised Corps (General-major Viktor T. Obukhov)
10th Tank Corps (General-major Vasily M. Alekseev)
52nd Army (General-leytenant Konstantin A. Koroteev)
73rd Rifle Corps (General-major Pavel F. Batitskii)
   136th Rifle Division
   254th Rifle Division
   294th Rifle Division
78th Rifle Corps (General-major Georgy A. Latyshev)
   93rd Rifle Division
   138th Rifle Division
   373rd Rifle Division
2nd Air Army (General-leytenant Stepan A. Krasovsky)
5th Fighter Aviation Corps
10th Fighter Aviation Corps
5th Ground Attack Aviation Corps
202nd Bomber Aviation Division
291st Ground Attack Aviation Division
Under front control:
4th Guards Tank Corps (General-leytenant Pavel P. Poluboyarov)
3rd Guards Mortar Division
13th Artillery Division
Provisional Airborne Corps
   1st Guards Airborne Brigade
   3rd Guards Airborne Brigade
   5th Guards Airborne Brigade
9th Guards Airborne Division
6th Pontoon Brigade

STEPPE FRONT (GENERAL-POLKOVNIK IVAN KONEV)
7th Guards Army (General-leytenant Mikhail S. Shumilov)
24th Guards Rifle Corps (General-major Nikolai A. Vasilev)
   72nd Guards Rifle Division
   213th Rifle Division
25th Guards Rifle Corps (General-major Ganii B. Safiulin)
   78th Guards Rifle Division
   81st Guards Rifle Division
49th Rifle Corps
   15th Guards Rifle Division
   111th Rifle Division
27th Guards Tank Brigade
201st Tank Brigade
5th Guards Tank Army (General-leytenant Pavel A. Rotmistrov)
18th Tank Corps (Polkovnik Aleksandr V. Egorov)
29th Tank Corps (General-major Ivan F. Kirichenko)

5th Guards Mechanised Corps (General-major Boris M. Skvortsov)

53rd Army (General-leytenant Ivan M. Managarov)

48th Rifle Corps (General-major Zinovi Z. Rogoznyi)

    107th Rifle Division

    116th Rifle Division

84th Rifle Division

214th Rifle Division

233rd Rifle Division

252nd Rifle Division

299th Rifle Division

16th Artillery Division

1st Mechanised Corps (General-leytenant Mikhail D. Solomatin)

57th Army (General-leytenant Nikolai A. Gagen)

27th Guards Rifle Corps (General-major Evgeny S. Alekhin)

    41st Guards Rifle Division

    58th Guards Rifle Division

64th Rifle Corps (General-major Mikhail B. Anashkin)

    14th Guards Rifle Division

    36th Guards Rifle Division

    52nd Rifle Division

68th Rifle Corps (General-major Nikolai N. Shkodunovich)

    19th Rifle Division

    113th Rifle Division

    303rd Rifle Division

173rd Tank Brigade

179th Tank Brigade

69th Army (General-leytenant Vasily D. Kriuchenkin)

35th Guards Rifle Corps (General-major Aleksandr N. Chernikov)

    93rd Guards Rifle Division

    183rd Rifle Division

89th Guards Rifle Division

94th Guards Rifle Division

305th Rifle Division

96th Tank Brigade

5th Air Army (General-leytenant Sergei K. Goriunov)

4th Fighter Aviation Corps

1st Bomber Aviation Corps

1st Ground Attack Aviation Corps

Under front control:

76th Rifle Corps

    28th Guards Rifle Division

    48th Guards Rifle Division

    375th Rifle Division

6th Pontoon Battalion

7th Pontoon Battalion

19th Pontoon Battalion

40th Pontoon Battalion

SOUTH-WESTERN FRONT (GENERAL RODION MALINOVSKY)

1st Guards Army (General-polkovnik Vasily I. Kuznetsov)

6th Guards Rifle Corps (General-major Ivan P. Alferov)

    44th Guards Rifle Division

    57th Guards Rifle Division

    195th Rifle Division

34th Rifle Corps (General-major Bogdan K. Kolchigin)

    6th Rifle Division

    24th Rifle Division

    152nd Rifle Division

    228th Rifle Division

20th Guards Rifle Division

2nd Guards Pontoon Battalion

3rd Guards Army (General-leytenant Dmitri D. Lelyushenko)

34th Guards Rifle Corps (General-major Nikolai M. Makovchuk)

    59th Guards Rifle Division

    61st Guards Rifle Division

    297th Rifle Division

32nd Rifle Corps (General-major Dmitri S. Zherebin)

    259th Rifle Division

    266th Rifle Division

    279th Rifle Division

8th Guards Army (General-leytenant Vasily I. Chuikov)

28th Guards Rifle Corps (General-major Stepan S. Gurev)

    39th Guards Rifle Division

    79th Guards Rifle Division

    88th Guards Rifle Division

29th Guards Rifle Corps (General-leytenant Iakov S. Fokanov)

    27th Guards Rifle Division

    74th Guards Rifle Division

    82nd Guards Rifle Division

6th Army (General-leytenant Ivan T. Shlemin)

4th Guards Rifle Corps (General-major Mikhail I. Zaporozhchenko)

    38th Guards Rifle Division

    263rd Rifle Division

    267th Rifle Division

26th Guards Rifle Corps (General-major Pavel A. Firsov)

    25th Guards Rifle Division

    35th Guards Rifle Division

    47th Guards Rifle Division

33rd Rifle Corps (General-major Mikhail I. Kozlov)

    50th Rifle Division

    78th Rifle Division

    243rd Rifle Division

12th Army (General-leytenant Aleksei I. Danilov)

66th Rifle Corps (General-major Dmitri A. Kupriianov)

    203rd Rifle Division

    244th Rifle Division

    333rd Rifle Division

67th Rifle Corps (General-major Dmitri I. Kislitsyn)

    60th Guards Rifle Division

    172nd Rifle Division

    350th Rifle Division

46th Army (General-major Vasily V. Glagolev)

31st Rifle Division

223rd Rifle Division

236th Rifle Division

353rd Rifle Division

394th Rifle Division

409th Rifle Division

17th Air Army (General-leytenant Vladimir A. Sudets)

1st Guards Composite Aviation Corps

1st Composite Aviation Corps

9th Composite Aviation Corps

244th Bomber Aviation Division

Under front control:

1st Guards Mechanised Corps (General-leytenant Ivan N. Russiyanov)

23rd Tank Corps (General-leytenant Efim G. Pushkin)

31st Guards Tank Brigade

11th Tank Brigade

115th Tank Brigade

7th Artillery Division

9th Artillery Division

4th Pontoon Brigade

5th Pontoon Brigade

8th Heavy Pontoon Regiment

SOUTHERN FRONT (GENERAL FYODOR I. TOLBUKHIN)

2nd Guards Army (General-leytenant Georgy F. Zakharov)

1st Guards Rifle Corps (General-leytenant Ivan I. Missan)

24th Guards Rifle Division

33rd Guards Rifle Division

86th Guards Rifle Division

13th Guards Rifle Corps (General-major Porfiriy G. Chanchibadze)

3rd Guards Rifle Division

49th Guards Rifle Division

87th Guards Rifle Division

151st Rifle Division

295th Rifle Division

2nd Guards Mechanised Corps (General-leytenant Karp V. Sviridov)

32nd Guards Tank Brigade

5th Shock Army (General-polkovnik Viacheslav D. Tsvetaev)

3rd Guards Rifle Corps (General-major Aleksandr I. Belov)

50th Guards Rifle Division

54th Guards Rifle Division

31st Guards Rifle Corps (General-major Aleksandr I. Utvenko)

4th Guards Rifle Division

34th Guards Rifle Division

40th Guards Rifle Division

96th Guards Rifle Division

9th Rifle Corps (General-major Ivan P. Roslyi)

230th Rifle Division

301st Rifle Division

320th Rifle Division

55th Rifle Corps (General-major Petr E. Loviagin)

87th Rifle Division

126th Rifle Division

99th Rifle Division

127th Rifle Division

271st Rifle Division

387th Rifle Division

28th Army (General-leytenant Vasily F. Gerasimenko)

37th Rifle Corps (General-major Sergei F. Gorokhov)

118th Rifle Division

248th Rifle Division

347th Rifle Division

416th Rifle Division

44th Army (General-leytenant Vasily A. Khomenko – fatally wounded 07.11.43; army disbanded)

130th Rifle Division

221st Rifle Division

51st Army (General-leytenant Iakov G. Kreizer)

10th Rifle Corps (General-major Konstantin P. Neverov)

216th Rifle Division

257th Rifle Division

328th Rifle Division

54th Rifle Corps (General-leytenant Trofim K. Kolomiets)

346th Rifle Division

63rd Rifle Corps (General-major Petr K. Koshevoi)

91st Rifle Division

315th Rifle Division

121st Pontoon Battalion

8th Air Army (General-leytenant Timofei T. Khriukhin)

3rd Fighter Aviation Corps

7th Ground Attack Aviation Corps

6th Guards Fighter Aviation Division

9th Guards Fighter Aviation Division

236th Fighter Aviation Division

270th Bomber Aviation Division

1st Guards Ground Attack Aviation Division

Under front control:

2nd Guards Artillery Division

4th Guards Mechanised Corps (General-leytenant Trofim I. Tanaschishin)

11th Tank Corps (General-major Nikolai N. Radkevich)

6th Guards Tank Brigade

33rd Guards Tank Brigade

1st Pontoon Brigade

2nd Pontoon Brigade

1st Pontoon Regiment

OPPOSING PLANS

GERMAN PLANS

The Red Army made effective use of nationalistic propaganda to motivate its troops. Here, a Ukrainian *izba* has been decorated with the slogan, 'Liberators of the Ukraine, forward, to the sacred banks of the Dnepr!' Local Ukrainian civilians were less enthusiastic about being immediately conscripted into the Red Army and used as cannon fodder in the breakout from the bridgeheads.

Hitler had been unwilling to consider the possibility of building fixed fortifications on the Eastern Front until after Operation *Zitadelle* had failed and it became obvious that the Wehrmacht was unable to defeat the Red Army. Despite devoting enormous material and labour resources to building the Atlantic Wall in the West, Hitler was loathe to put even a fraction of this effort into construction of fortifications in the East since it implied a loss of strategic initiative. Nor was Hitler willing to abandon his position in the Kuban, where he kept 17.Armee until October 1943. Even after calling off *Zitadelle* and transferring troops from Heeresgruppe Süd to deal with the Allied landings in Sicily, Hitler was opposed to officially shifting to a defensive strategy in the East. Von Manstein and other senior generals pleaded with Hitler to abandon the Kuban and build defences behind the Dnepr, but were ignored. Then, at the eleventh hour, Hitler finally agreed to the construction of the Panther–Wotan-Stellung extending from the Baltic to the Black Sea. This was a gargantuan task and Organisation Todt had only begun site preparation at a few locations when the German retreat began and the line was little more than a concept when the Red Army arrived.

In order to get behind the Dnepr, Heeresgruppe Süd's armies had to break contact with the Red Army and retreat 100 or more kilometres to a handful of crossing sites. Hoth was ordered to retreat to Kiev, Kanev and Cherkassy. Wöhler's 8.Armee was ordered to cross at Kremenchug, while von Mackensen's 1. Panzerarmee would cross at Dnepropetrovsk and Zaporozhe. The retreat would be handicapped by having to cross the Dnepr at only a small number of bridges, which were vulnerable to enemy bombing. Once German units reached the Dnepr, they then had to rapidly fan out and dig themselves in, creating fieldworks near possible enemy crossing sites. Yet Hitler was not willing to abandon the eastern banks of the Dnepr and hide behind a river; instead, he ordered that Heeresgruppe Süd would maintain several

bridgeheads across the Dnepr to facilitate future German offensives. In Hitler's self-deceiving mind, the Panther-Stellung along the Dnepr would provide an 'Eastern bulwark' to stop any further Soviet advances, enabling the Third Reich to maintain its grip on the western Ukraine and the Crimea.

Hollidt's 6.Armee was ordered to retreat to Melitopol, where it would have to defend this position forward of the Dnepr in order to protect the rail line from Kherson heading into the Crimea. Hitler obstinately refused to abandon the Crimea, which denied 6.Armee the benefit of defending behind the Dnepr. The terrain in this area was fairly flat and open – very good tank country – and poorly suited for defence. Thus, the requirement to maintain a rail line of communications seriously weakened the Panther-Stellung concept from the start. Hitler finally agreed to evacuate 17.Armee from the Kuban, but rather than transferring it to reinforce the defences on the Dnepr, he instead ordered it to hold the Crimea.

Hitler's intention to create an Eastern bulwark along the Dnepr was compromised from the start by lack of prior planning and inadequate forces in place to execute the mission. However, if Hitler had ordered creation of the Panther-Stellung prior to *Zitadelle* and evacuated 17.Armee from the Kuban and the Crimea, then used it to garrison the line, the situation might have been very different. Under those circumstances, von Manstein's retreating armies would have been able to fall back upon prepared, manned defensive positions, which would have presented the Soviets with circumstances akin to that facing the Western Allies along the Rhine River in March 1945. Axis-allied units, including the remaining Romanian and Hungarian infantry, could also have been used to supplement 17.Armee-held positions behind the Dnepr – but they were virtually ignored in German planning. If nothing else, a serious defensive effort along the Dnepr would likely have thwarted most Soviet ad hoc crossing efforts and forced the Red Army to mount time-consuming, deliberate assault crossing operations. Rather than opining about 'what ifs', the point here is that a professionally planned and executed defence behind the Dnepr offered one last potential chance for Germany to achieve a temporary stalemate on the Eastern Front. Hitler's increasingly irrational style of decision-making made even this impossible.

Once the retreat to the Dnepr commenced, Hitler began to lose interest in the Eastern Front because he knew that the prospect for any further major victories was slim. He also knew that the Western Allies would likely mount an invasion of France in 1944 and he believed that defeating such an attempt would mean more to the survival of his regime than the retention of obscure Ukrainian towns. Thus, on 3 November Hitler issued Führer Directive 51, which gave priority of reinforcements and replacements to the forces in the West. From this point on, the Eastern Front was no longer the German main effort, and consequently Heeresgruppe Süd was condemned to an unequal battle of attrition.

This was one of the strongest parts of Hitler's vaunted Panther-Stellung – some hastily dug infantry fighting positions overlooking a crossing point on the Dnepr. These types of shallow positions offered no real protection against large-scale Soviet artillery bombardments – which would not be long in coming. (Author's collection)

SOVIET PLANS

Gaining bridgeheads across the Dnepr River was the holy grail for Stavka strategic planning after Stalingrad, against which all other major offensive plans were measured – the critical question being, would the operation in question get the Red Army across the Dnepr or not? Stavka believed – rightly so – that once across the Dnepr, there would be no significant terrain obstacle that could stop the Red Army from liberating the rest of the Ukraine. Initial planning efforts in February 1943 were simplistic and simply hoped that Vatutin's armoured units would somehow capture a crossing site over the Dnepr, but the offensive outran its logistic support before it even reached the river. After the battle of Kursk, Marshal Georgy Zhukov worked with Vatutin in developing a rough plan to get to the Dnepr with enough combat power to cross the river at multiple points. However, the Stavka planning remained fairly generalised and avoided irksome details. Indeed, initially no main effort was designated – all five fronts involved would simply advance as rapidly towards the Dnepr as possible. Nor did Stavka make any special effort to allocate additional engineer bridging units or logistic support to the fronts involved in the Lower Dnepr operation – they would simply have to make do with available resources. In this regard, and in the employment of airborne forces to assist with crossing efforts, Soviet operational-level planning was slipshod.

Zhukov and Stavka agreed upon the desired end state of securing multiple crossings over the Dnepr, but the actual execution was dictated by opportunistic orders. The liberation of Kiev was an obvious objective, but the method of accomplishing this was left to Vatutin and his staff to figure out. Consequently, the lack of detailed planning led to difficulty in exploiting the initial bridgeheads and then a shifting of priorities during the campaign as some bridgeheads proved more useful than others. Soviet planning did improve as the campaign progressed and the Dnepr was crossed, with a demonstrated ability to concentrate combat power into a main effort, then use deception and manoeuvre to achieve their objectives. However, the lack of priority afforded to logistic planning until Soviet forces were engaged across the Dnepr seriously undermined the ability of the Red Army to exploit the initial crossing operations.

German troops were stunned when they found no prepared positions waiting for them behind the Dnepr River. Instead, they were forced to occupy hasty defensive positions, like this MG 34 team. (Author's collection)

THE CAMPAIGN

SEPTEMBER: RACE FOR THE DNEPR

Although von Manstein's attention was focused on the incessant Soviet pounding on his front from Akhtyrka to the Sea of Azov, the real trouble came on his left flank, near the boundary with Heeresgruppe Mitte. After the loss of Orel, Generaloberst Walter Model's 9.Armee had conducted a successful fighting withdrawal to the Hagen-Stellung, located behind the Desna River. Unlike the Panther-Stellung, the Hagen-Stellung was a real defensive position that Model had ordered constructed prior to *Zitadelle* and now it was sufficiently strong to halt the pursuing Soviet armies. Yet while Model's forces were temporarily secure, General der Infanterie Walter Weiss' 2.Armee, which consisted of two corps with six depleted infantry divisions, was forced to remain in open terrain around Sevsk to maintain the link with Hoth's 4.Panzerarmee. In order to stiffen Weiss' defence, Model transferred the LVI Panzerkorps with the 4., 8. and 12. Panzer divisions, but these divisions were severely understrength and altogether had fewer than 100 tanks and assault guns. Temporarily stymied by the Hagen-Stellung, Rokossovsky's Central Front shifted its axis of attack from pursuing Model to focusing most of its combat power against Weiss' vulnerable army. On 26 August Rokossovsky attacked with his infantry and, despite the efforts of the LVI Panzerkorps, quickly achieved a breakthrough near Sevsk with the 38th and 60th armies. Rokossovsky wasted no time before inserting General-leytenant Semyon Bogdanov's 2nd Tank Army (consisting of 3rd and 16th

The Germans blew up most of the bridges over the Dnepr just before the Red Army arrived, including the railway bridge at Kremenchug, shown here. (Author's collection)

German retreat to the Dnepr and initial Soviet pursuit, 15–23 September 1943.

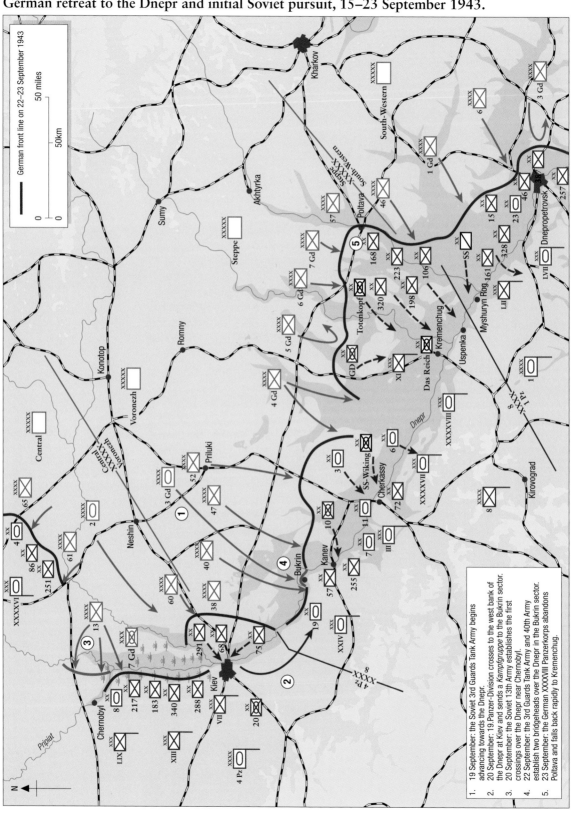

1. 19 September: the Soviet 3rd Guards Tank Army begins advancing towards the Dnepr.
2. 20 September: 19.Panzer-Division crosses to the west bank of the Dnepr at Kiev and sends a *Kampfgruppe* to the Bukrin sector.
3. 20 September: the Soviet 13th Army establishes the first crossings over the Dnepr near Chernobyl.
4. 22 September: the 3rd Guards Tank Army and 40th Army establish two bridgeheads over the Dnepr in the Bukrin sector.
5. 23 September: the German XXXVIII Panzerkorps abandons Poltava and falls back rapidly to Kremenchug.

Tank corps, and 7th Guards Mechanised Corps) into the breach, which created a 60km-deep penetration and split apart Heeresgruppe Mitte from Heeresgruppe Süd. By early September, Weiss' 2.Armee was retreating to the Desna, exposing Hoth's left flank.

Rokossovsky's breakthrough not only unhinged von Manstein's defensive efforts east of the Dnepr, but Bogdanov's 2nd Tank Army was already within 120km of Kiev. The only major unit in Kiev was the 213.Sicherungs-Division, which was intended to fight partisans, not tank armies. Due to the pressure all along his front, von Manstein was not in a position to transfer any armour to his left flank to assist Weiss since it was all concentrated in the centre around Poltava and on the right near Stalino. Hoth's vulnerable left flank was held by three infantry corps, which had limited mobility and firepower. The LVI Panzerkorps refused its flank in front of Bogdanov's 2nd Tank Army and used 12.Panzer-Division to conduct a delaying action, but the Soviet tank army continued to advance towards the south-west. Consequently, the defeat of Weiss' 2.Armee made it imperative that von Manstein's entire Heeresgruppe Süd retreat to the Dnepr before Rokossovsky's Central Front bounced the river and captured a lightly defended Kiev.

In great haste, the OKH transferred Generalleutnant Otto Lasch's 217. Infanterie-Division from Heeresgruppe Nord to Kiev by express train. The division began unloading near Neshin on 10 September. Lasch's division had been involved in the siege of Leningrad since 1941 and now it was suddenly thrown in the path of a major Soviet offensive. It was joined by 8.Panzer-Division and together these two divisions formed a hedgehog around Neshin, 115km north-east of Kiev. Meanwhile, Rokossovsky's forces lunged towards the Dnepr, with General-leytenant Nikolai P. Pukhov's 13th Army in the lead. Pukhov's army had borne the brunt of stopping Model's offensive during *Zitadelle*, but was now in a position to demonstrate its offensive capabilities.

Yet rather than taking the direct path through Neshin to Kiev, Pukhov's army advanced cross-country into a gap where there were no major German units. On 21 September, the 70th Guards Rifle Division from the 17th Guards Rifle Corps reached the Dnepr near Teremtsy, 86km north of Kiev. With no German troops in the area, two regiments began crossing the 400m-wide Dnepr on rafts and anything else that floated. Although the Germans were in no position to oppose the initial crossing, both Lasch's 217.Infanterie-Division and 8.Panzer-Division were ordered to force-march west to Chernobyl to block Pukhov's bridgeheads. On the next day, Pukhov's two other rifle corps reached the Dnepr and the 181st Rifle Division began crossing near Mnevo (100km north of Kiev) and the 8th Rifle Division near Navozy. Meanwhile, the 70th Guards Rifle Division boldly advanced 9km to seize a crossing over the

Heavily armed Soviet troops in a posed photo. Small boats like these were sometimes used in the Dnepr crossing, but not until engineer units reached the river. (From the fonds of the RGAKFD in Krasnogorsk via Stavka)

Soviet infantrymen conducting a river crossing in small craft. Vessels like this were highly vulnerable to automatic weapons fire, but the initial Soviet crossings of the Dnepr were mostly at night and unopposed. (From the fonds of the RGAKFD in Krasnogorsk via Stavka)

Pripiat River at Otashev. By the time that Lasch's division began to reach this sector on 22/23 September, Pukhov had already seized a 35km-deep bridgehead over the Dnepr and had elements of five rifle divisions across.

On 15 September, the bulk of Heeresgruppe Süd had begun withdrawing to the Dnepr, but von Manstein was forced to conduct a major delaying action around Poltava to slow the Soviet pursuit. The delaying action at Poltava involved most of Hoth's armour, including four Panzer divisions (3., 6., 7. and 11.) and four Panzer-grenadier divisions ('Wiking', 'Das Reich', 'Totenkopf' and 'Grossdeutschland') from III and XXXXVIII Panzerkorps.[2] Consequently, very little German armour was available to protect the six main crossing sites over the Dnepr. The sole exception was Oberst Hans Källner's 19.Panzer-Division, which crossed the Dnepr at Kiev on 20 September – the first of von Manstein's armoured units to regain the western bank. Källner's division had been gutted in recent fighting and Hoth directed it to assemble as a mobile reserve in Kiev where it could receive replacements; the reconnaissance battalion, however, was sent to screen the river south of the city, which was undefended. In addition, General der Panzertruppen Walther Nehring's XXIV Panzerkorps was ordered to cross the Dnepr at Kanev in order to provide a rapid defence force on the western bank. Nehring, one of the most experienced German Panzer commanders, had 10.Panzergrenadier-Division, Sturmgeschütz-Abteilung 239 and elements of three battered infantry divisions under his command. These German units all had to transit the Dnepr over a few bridges, then fan out rapidly along the river to cover potential crossing sites that the Soviets might use.

The German retreat itself was chaotic, with a great deal of equipment being abandoned or blown up. Discipline slipped, as troops looted supply dumps that were about to be torched, including stockpiles of liquor. In accord with Hitler's scorched earth policy, troops also burned villages and farms, while German pioneers blew up factories and tore up rail lines. Thousands of Ukrainian civilians and their livestock were also herded westwards, to keep them out of the hands of the Red Army. As the great retreat began, heavy rains fell, turning many of the unpaved roads into muddy morasses and further depressing German front-line morale. While scorched earth tactics are a contravention of international conventions on warfare, it should be noted that the Red Army had itself employed similar tactics when it retreated from the Dnepr in 1941. On 18 August that year, NKVD personnel had blown up the Zaporozhe hydroelectric dam; the resulting flood drowned at least 20,000 local Ukrainians, possibly more.

2   11. Panzer-Division, under Generalmajor Wend von Wietersheim, was initially assigned to XXXXVIII Panzerkorps. Its status during the retreat remains unclear.

Meanwhile, Vatutin's Voronezh Front was a day behind Rokossovsky's Central Front in reaching the Dnepr because it had to fight its way through Hoth's rearguards. The 27th and 40th armies had difficulty pushing past Hoth's left flank towards the Dnepr, but it was Stavka's decision to transfer General-polkovnik Pavel S. Rybalko's 3rd Guards Tank Army (6th and 7th Guards Tank corps, and 9th Mechanised Corps) to Vatutin that energised the pursuit. Rybalko's 3rd Guards Tank Army had been brought out of reserve and positioned near Sumy when it was given the mission of spearheading Vatutin's drive to the Dnepr. Although Rybalko's tank brigades were only at about half strength and short on fuel, they were full of fight. After receiving his orders from Vatutin, Rybalko's 3rd Guards Tank Army began advancing towards the Dnepr on the night of 19/20 September. Podpolkovnik Trofim F. Malik's 56th Guards Tank Brigade was in the lead as the advance guard. In a single day, Rybalko's tank army advanced 165km and by the evening of 21 September, Malik's tanks were approaching the Dnepr. Vatutin had selected the 'Dnepr Knee', a great bend in the river 80km south-east of Kiev, as his primary crossing site since Soviet partisans reported no German troops in this area. Stavka confirmed Vatutin's choice, since they assessed that the Germans would have strong defences at all of the five primary crossing sites over the Dnepr – which soon proved to be a false assumption.

Malik's tanks were nearly within sight of the river when they began to run out of fuel. General-major Mitrofan I. Zin'kovich, commander of the 6th Guards Tank Corps, frantically radioed Rybalko and requested an emergency fuel resupply of 20–30t of diesel for his T-34s; it would take some time for the fuel trucks to arrive. With the tanks temporarily immobilised, the Soviet infantry who had been carried on Malik's tanks jumped off and began walking to the river. A submachine-gun company, with fewer than 100 troops, reached the river and found a few small boats, which they used to begin crossing at Grigorovka. At this point, the Dnepr was 600–800m wide and 8m deep. As more troops arrived, they began to cross as well and by dawn on 22 September, Rybalko had a battalion-size force across the Dnepr. Around the same time, elements of the 237th and 309th Rifle divisions from General-polkovnik Kirill S. Moskalenko's 40th Army reached the Dnepr near Rzhyshchiv, 25km to the west. Moskalenko's infantrymen also began to cross the river using rafts and small boats. These two tiny Soviet bridgeheads were in heavily wooded areas and not within supporting distance, but initially the only German troops in this area were a few detachments from Sicherungs-Regiment 602.

Soviet sub-machine gunners cross a river in small boats. With a handful of craft such as these, it could take most of a night to move a single battalion across the Dnepr. Furthermore, it is clear that small boats such as these could not carry heavy weapons or significant amounts of supplies. (Courtesy of the Central Museum of the Armed Forces, Moscow via Stavka)

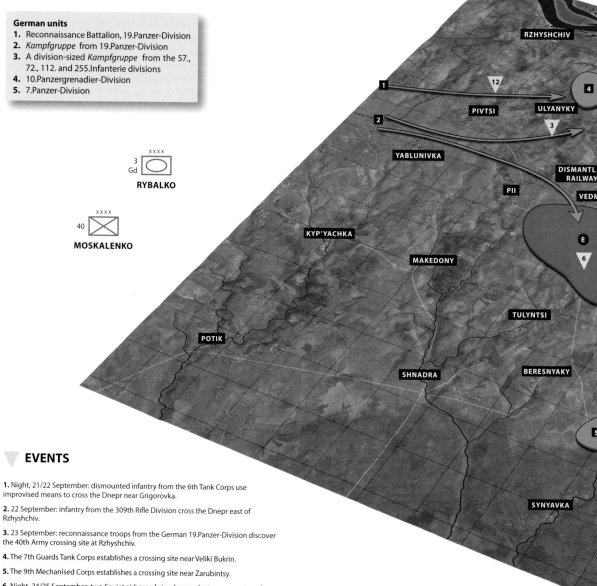

German units
1. Reconnaissance Battalion, 19.Panzer-Division
2. *Kampfgruppe* from 19.Panzer-Division
3. A division-sized *Kampfgruppe* from the 57., 72., 112. and 255.Infanterie divisions
4. 10.Panzergrenadier-Division
5. 7.Panzer-Division

3 Gd
RYBALKO

40
MOSKALENKO

RZHYSHCHIV
PIVTSI
ULYANYKY
YABLUNIVKA
DISMANTL RAILWAY
PII
VEDM
KYP'YACHKA
MAKEDONY
E
6
TULYNTSI
POTIK
BERESNYAKY
SHNADRA
SYNYAVKA

▼ EVENTS

1. Night, 21/22 September: dismounted infantry from the 6th Tank Corps use improvised means to cross the Dnepr near Grigorovka.

2. 22 September: infantry from the 309th Rifle Division cross the Dnepr east of Rzhyshchiv.

3. 23 September: reconnaissance troops from the German 19.Panzer-Division discover the 40th Army crossing site at Rzhyshchiv.

4. The 7th Guards Tank Corps establishes a crossing site near Veliki Bukrin.

5. The 9th Mechanised Corps establishes a crossing site near Zarubintsy.

6. Night, 24/25 September: two Soviet airborne brigades conduct a very scattered drop west of Kanev. The 19.Panzer-Division overruns some of the drop zones, inflicting heavy losses. Surviving paratroopers either link up with local partisans or escape to try and reach the Soviet bridgeheads near Bukrin.

7. 25–26 September: after mopping up the Soviet paratroopers, 19.Panzer-Division advances to form blocking positions near Romashky and Malyi Bukrin.

8. 26 September: a mixed formation including *Kampfgruppen* from the 57., 72., 112. and 255.Infanterie divisions moves north from Kanev to block Soviet expansion out of the Bukrin bridgeheads.

9. 26–28 September: the 40th Army seizes two more small bridgeheads across the Dnepr.

10. 26 September: the first Soviet pontoon engineers reach the Dnepr and begin ferrying Rybalko's tanks across. Elements of the 27th Army also cross into the Bukrin bridgehead.

11. 27–28 September: with limited armour support, the small Bukrin bridgeheads expand and create a front across the base of the 'Dnepr Knee'.

12. 28 September: 10.Panzergrenadier-Division arrives to contain the 40th Army bridgeheads.

13. 28 September: 7.Panzer-Division arrives to assist the counter-attack against the Soviet crossing sites.

14. 29 September: the Germans mount a counter-attack against the Bukrin bridgehead but fail to dislodge the Soviet forces, which are now reinforced with tanks and anti-tank guns.

15. 30 September: after a week, Vatutin's forces have finally linked up many of the small bridgeheads and created a front. The next task is to break out of the Bukrin bridgehead.

FIGHT FOR THE BUKRIN BRIDGEHEAD, 21–29 SEPTEMBER 1943

Vatutin sent Rybalko's 3rd Guards Tank Army and Moskalenko's 40th Army racing towards the 'Dnepr Knee', which was believed to be unguarded. Before the Germans could react, Vatutin's vanguard seized several crossing sites over the Dnepr. However, Nehring's XXIV Panzerkorps arrived just as the Soviets were ready to mount an airborne operation to enlarge their bridgeheads.

SOVIET UNITS
A. 6th Tank Corps
B. 309th Rifle Division
C. 7th Guards Tank Corps
D. 9th Mechanised Corps
E. 10th Guards Airborne Brigade
F. 5th Guards Airborne Brigade
G. 68th Guards Rifle Division
H. 253rd Rifle Division
I. 337th Rifle Division
J. 38th Rifle Division
K. 161st Rifle Division

BALYKO-
CHUCHYNKA

TRAKTOMIROV

ZARUBINTSY

VELIKI BUKRIN

KHODOROV

LUKOVYTSYA

ROMASHKY

SHEVO

TUNNEL

CHERNYSHI

GRIGOROVKA

IVANKIV

BUCHAK

TROSHCHYN

GRYSCHYNTSI

DNEPR RIVER

BOBRYTSYA

SELISHCHE

TROSTYANETS

KOVALI

XXX
XXIV ⬭
NEHRING

LYTVINETS

KOSTYANETS

KANEV

N

41

For about 24 hours, the Germans had no idea that Vatutin's forces had crossed the Dnepr. Källner's 19. Panzer-Division was still assembling in Kiev but it sent Rittmeister Helmut von Moltke's Panzer-Aufklärungs-Abteilung 19 to monitor the Dnepr south of Kiev. The Germans were aware that the Dnepr Knee offered potential crossing sites and intended to deploy forces to defend this sector as soon as practical. On the afternoon of 23 September, von Moltke's reconnaissance troops encountered Moskalenko's bridgehead near Rzhyshchiv and realised that

Soviet engineers have lashed three boats together and laid floorboards across the top to create a ferry across the Dnepr. The Soviets were quick to establish ferry points across the Dnepr, but the Luftwaffe was also quick to identify and bomb these sites, which made crossings hazardous in daylight. (Courtesy of the Central Museum of the Armed Forces, Moscow via Stavka)

Vatutin had already crossed the Dnepr. Hoth immediately ordered Källner to send a reinforced *Kampfgruppe* (two Panzergrenadier battalions, one artillery battalion and one tank company) to counter-attack the bridgehead. Hoth also ordered Nehring's XXIV Panzerkorps, which was beginning to cross the bridge at Kanev, to send a *Kampfgruppe* from 57.Infanterie-Division to assist Källner's counter-attack. By this point, Hoth had to deal with a major Soviet crossing north of Kiev and smaller crossings south of Kiev, even though the bulk of 4.Panzerarmee was still east of the Dnepr. With limited resources available, Hoth had to make hard choices. He abandoned the strongpoint at Neshin, which allowed Vatutin's main body to rapidly advance towards Kiev. The XIII Armeekorps fought a rearguard action east of the Dnepr to buy time for slower elements to cross, but it was clear that Hoth lacked the troops to hold a bridgehead on the eastern bank as Hitler had stipulated.

Soviet troops attempt to float an anti-tank gun across a river on a flimsy raft that is just below the surface. Soviet infantrymen also used telephone poles and trees to cross the Dnepr. Most of the initial crossing was conducted with such ad hoc means and some of these efforts must have come to grief. (From the fonds of the RGAKFD in Krasnogorsk via Stavka)

Meanwhile, Rybalko and Moskalenko were struggling to get as many troops across the Dnepr before the Germans could mount a counter-attack. Rybalko could not get any of his tanks across until the first engineer bridging units arrived, but on the night of 23/24 September he and Moskalenko sent several thousand troops across on rafts and boats. Some daring troops swam across the Dnepr. The 7th Guards Tank Corps seized a crossing at Veliki Bukrin, while the 9th Mechanised Corps crossed at Zarubintsy. Although this influx of troops allowed the Bukrin bridgehead to expand to a depth of 3–4km, the troops were very lightly armed and had little food or ammunition. Nor did they have any anti-aircraft defences. Reconnaissance flights by Ju 88D aircraft from 2.(F)/100 quickly identified the Soviet crossing sites near Bukrin and bombers arrived after dawn on 24 September to attack them. General-major Zin'kovich had crossed into the bridgehead and he was one of the first casualties of the Luftwaffe air raids, which soon made crossing in daylight difficult.

While Rokossovsky and Vatutin expanded their bridgeheads, Hoth could do little more than attempt to contain them. An effort by 8.Panzer-Division to move against Pukhov's 13th Army stalled near Chernobyl and steadily lost ground. On 24 September, Cherniakhovsky's 60th Army began crossing at Domantova, south of Pukhov's 13th Army lodgement, which threatened to outflank 8.Panzer-Division's strongpoint at Chernobyl. Only the timely arrival of Lasch's 217.Infanterie-Division and other units from the LIX Armeekorps limited Cherniakhovsky's lodgement. A *Kampfgruppe* from 5.Panzer-Division struck the northern side of Pukhov's lodgement, inflicting heavy losses on the 70th Guards Rifle Division. However, Pukhov managed to get armour from the 129th Tank Brigade and 29th Guards Tank Regiment across the Dnepr, which halted the German counter-attack.

By midday on 24 September, it was clear that both Rokossovsky and Vatutin were across the Dnepr River at multiple points. Unknown to von Manstein, Zhukov and Stavka decided that the time was right to employ a large-scale airborne landing to support the main effort, Vatutin's Front. Earlier Soviet airborne operations in 1941–42 had been hastily thrown together, and this time was no different. The basic plan was to drop three airborne brigades near Kanev to help Vatutin's forces expand the Bukrin bridgehead, but the haphazard planning effort by Vatutin's staff ignored the enemy and the limited availability of air transport. Amazingly, Vatutin planned to insert the paratroops across a 70km-wide swathe between

German infantry dig in around the initial Soviet bridgeheads across the Dnepr and attempt to contain them. German troops were severely disappointed that there were no prepared positions on the vaunted Panther-Stellung and front-line morale suffered. By this point, it was obvious to even the most junior soldiers that the war in the East was not going well. (HITM)

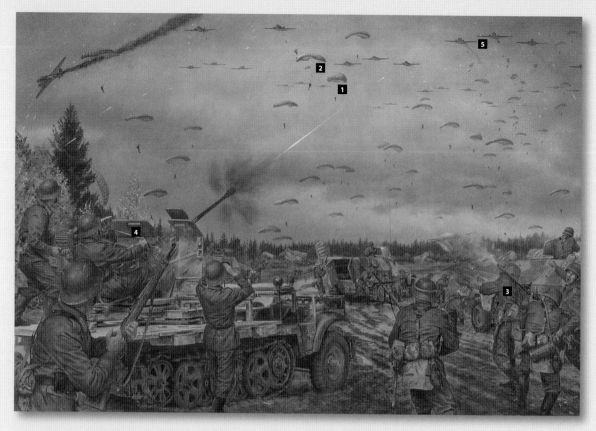

SOVIET PARATROOPERS JUMP NEAR KANEV, EVENING 24 SEPTEMBER 1943 (PP. 44–45)

Since spring 1943, Stavka had been training several airborne brigades for a potential large-scale airborne operation to be conducted when conditions were favourable. As Vatutin's forces approached the Dnepr River in late September, Stavka believed that an airborne operation could assist the Red Army in rapidly securing a lodgement across the river. Vatutin was provided with three airborne brigades but there was only sufficient transport aircraft to fly in parts of two brigades. Although the concept was fine, the planning was badly bungled and weather interfered with the drops, which resulted in the Soviet paratroopers being dropped in piecemeal fashion and over too large an area. Even worse, many Soviet paratroopers landed on top of Panzergrenadier-Regiment 73, which was just arriving in the Kanev sector. The Soviet paratroops jumped with only light arms, usually a submachine gun with two drums and a couple of grenades; they depended upon reaching their supply canisters which contained machine guns, mortars and radios. Officers jumped with the oval PD-6 parachute (**1**), but enlisted soldiers

used the square PD-41 parachute (**2**). In this operation, Soviet paratroops dropped from 300m.

Here, German Panzergrenadiers (**3**) are engaging paratroopers from the first wave of the 3rd Guards Airborne Brigade with automatic weapons. An attached flak gun (**4**) is firing at one of the Li-2 transports (**5**). Since the Germans controlled most of the drop zones, the Soviet supply and weapons containers could not be retrieved. While the Germans eliminated roughly one-fifth of the paratroopers on the first day, the survivors escaped into the adjoining forests with little or no equipment. Some linked up with local partisans, others reached Soviet lines many weeks later. Nevertheless, the Soviet airborne drop was a disaster that resulted in the destruction of two elite brigades without providing any real assistance to Vatutin's efforts to expand the Bukrin bridgehead. After this debacle, the Red Army had no further interest in attempting to conduct large-scale airborne operations for the rest of World War II.

Rzhyshchiv and Kanev, rather than concentrate them to seize a specific objective. The rainy weather then inflicted a critical 24-hour delay and the shortage of fuel for the transport aircraft meant that only part of two brigades could be dropped, instead of three. Furthermore, the transports had to take off in small groups and then return to the airfields to load the next group of paratroops, which meant that even dropping two brigades would take many hours.

Previous Soviet airborne operations had occurred at night, but the Dnepr airborne operation began in daylight. Due to faulty planning, electronic navigational beacons were not installed in time and the inadequately trained Soviet transport aircrews had difficulty finding the drop zones near Rzhyshchiv and Kanev due to overcast weather and haze. The drop of the 3rd and 5th Guards Airborne brigades began at 1930hrs, just 24 minutes before sunset. From the outset, the drops were badly scattered and got worse once darkness fell; only one-quarter of the paratroops would land within 10km of their intended drop zones. Sergeant Petr N. Nezhivenko, from 3rd Guards Airborne Brigade, jumped from 300m and later discovered that he had missed his intended drop zone

Soviet paratroopers jump during training. During the Kanev airborne operation, the drops were widely scattered due to navigational problems and the spacing of individual paratroopers was often much greater. Soviet paratroops packed their heavier automatic weapons and mortars into canisters, but few were recovered from the drop zones, leaving the airborne troops only lightly armed. (Author's collection)

by 25–30km. By the fortunes of war, a *Kampfgruppe* from 19.Panzer-Division had just arrived from Kiev to reinforce von Moltke's hard-pressed reconnaissance battalion and many of the Soviet paratroopers landed virtually on top of Panzergrenadier-Regiment 73. German troops engaged the descending paratroopers with automatic weapons and light flak guns, inflicting great slaughter. Then the Panzergrenadiers moved in to mop up the survivors. As more Soviet transports arrived during the night, the Germans fired off flares, which led to more paratroops landing near German positions. Altogether, 4,575 Soviet paratroopers were dropped near Bukrin by dawn on 25 September; over 200 landed behind Soviet lines and the Germans captured or killed 901 of them in the first 24 hours. Eventually, several groups of

A larger Soviet engineer raft, created from pontoon bridging material, carrying a 45t SU-152 self-propelled gun across the Dnepr. This was a slow and tedious process, vulnerable to Luftwaffe attack; however, until the large pontoon bridges were built across the Dnepr, such methods were necessary. (Courtesy of the Central Museum of the Armed Forces, Moscow via Stavka)

paratroopers coalesced in wooded areas in the German rear, but they had little ammunition or heavy weapons. Some, like Sergeant Nezhivenko, opted to join the partisans and about 1,000 eventually fought their way through to Soviet lines, but the two brigades were essentially destroyed. In short, the Soviet Dnepr airborne operation was a complete disaster.

In contrast to Vatutin's rapid advance to the Dnepr, Konev's Steppe Front was forced to mount a set-piece offensive. The German III and XXXXVIII Panzerkorps conducted a desperate delaying action near Poltava until 23 September, when they finally abandoned the city. Thanks to the rearguard action, Wöhler's slow-moving 8.Armee was able to cross the Dnepr unmolested at Cherkassy and Kremenchug. However, once Wöhler's infantry was safely across, most of the German mechanised divisions had to bolt for the river, with III Panzerkorps heading to Cherkassy and XXXXVIII Panzerkorps going to Kremenchug. At the bridge sites, German convoys bunched up into huge traffic jams and German soldiers were amazed that the Soviet VVS did not bomb these packed targets. In fact, the VVS did attempt to mount a few raids against railway bridges, but were often deterred by German flak defences around the Dnepr bridges. On 21 September, a group of eight Il-2 Sturmoviks from the 3rd Guards Ground Attack Aviation Regiment managed to damage the railway bridge at Zaporozhe, but the group leader was shot down in the process. Doctrinally, the VVS did not often conduct 'battlefield interdiction sorties' because Soviet army-level commanders had little interest in distant operations and instead preferred that their Air Armies commit most of their aircraft to supporting their own ground operations. In the Red Army, the lack of an independent air force made it difficult to employ airpower in roles that took resources away from the ground battle.

Amazingly, Konev's vanguard was able to bypass the retreating German mechanised units and reach the Dnepr first. On the night of 25/26 September, troops from the 7th Guards Army managed to cross the Dnepr at Uspenka, south of Kremenchug. Two days later, another crossing was seized at Deriyivka. Konev's initial bridgeheads were small and not connected, but

Soviet troops crossing a river on very flimsy rafts. It is unlikely that enemy troops are in the vicinity, since the survivability of these troops should they come under automatic weapons or mortar fire would be nil. Using such methods, the Red Army was able to move large numbers of troops across the Dnepr in late September 1943. (From the fonds of the RGAKFD in Krasnogorsk via Stavka)

In time, Soviet engineers built proper pontoon bridges across the Dnepr, which allowed tanks, trucks and artillery to build up rapidly on the west bank. Although the Luftwaffe damaged several pontoon bridges, they failed to interdict Soviet supply lines across the Dnepr. (Courtesy of the Central Museum of the Armed Forces, Moscow via Stavka)

Wöhler's 8.Armee had few troops available to contain them. The only nearby unit was a *Kampfgruppe* from 106.Infanterie-Division, which lacked the infantry strength to create a continuous perimeter around the bridgeheads. Konev's bridgeheads over the Dnepr were near the boundary of 8.Armee and Mackensen's 1.Panzerarmee, so von Manstein directed the latter to send reinforcements to this sector. After some delay, Mackensen was able to position the SS-Kavallerie-Division and *Kampfgruppen* from 23.Panzer-Division and Panzergrenadier-Division 'Grossdeutschland' to try to block any expansion of Konev's bridgeheads.

Further south, von Mackensen's forces retreated to Dnepropetrovsk where most of his 1.Panzerarmee was able to cross without difficulty. However, Hitler directed that 1.Panzerarmee would maintain a bridgehead on the east bank of the Dnepr near Zaporozhe, in order to protect the dams and hydroelectric power plants. As usual, whenever a region with economic value was threatened, Hitler refused to allow the army to abandon it without a fight. Von Mackensen was forced to leave six divisions of Generaloberst Gotthard Heinrici's XXXX Panzerkorps, including 9.Panzer-Division, on the east bank to protect the approaches to the Dnepr dam. There were no prepared defensive positions in this sector, which consisted of essentially flat terrain. Although he had precious few tanks to protect the west side of the Dnepr, von Mackensen was forced to commit the remnants of schwere Panzerjäger-Regiment 656 and Sturmpanzer-Abteilung 216, consisting of 12 repaired Ferdinands and 13 Sturmpanzers, to reinforce Heinrici's corps in the Zaporozhe bridgehead. Von Manstein also diverted his only significant reinforcement in this period – Major Gerhard Willing's schwere Panzer-Abteilung 506 just arrived from Germany with 45 new Tigers – to reinforce Heinrici's bridgehead. In short order, Malinovsky's 3rd and 8th Guards armies converged upon Heinrici's corps and prepared to pound it into dust.

Soviet engineers constructing a tactical bridge. The Red Army's engineers and combat support troops never received the attention lavished on tank, rifle and airborne units, but they played an increasingly vital role as Soviet forces advanced westwards. (From the fonds of the RGAKFD in Krasnogorsk via Stavka)

At the southern end of the illusory Panther–Wotan-Stellung, Hollidt's 6.Armee had withdrawn behind the Molochna River around Melitopol by 20 September. Aside from the minor water obstacle to their front, this area consisted of flat farmland and was unsuited to a protracted defence. Hollidt's corps was now subordinate to von Kleist's Heeresgruppe A and was ordered to hold Melitopol in order to maintain a rail link to 17.Armee in the Crimea. Von Manstein recognised that the Crimea should be abandoned and Heeresgruppe A should pull back to the Dnepr, but Hitler absolutely refused. Hollidt's exhausted troops began digging in, but within a few days Tolbukhin's pursuing forces arrived. Tolbukhin wasted no time and launched a large-scale hasty attack with the 5th Shock Army and 44th Army against Hollidt's left flank on 26 September. This sector was held by IV Armeekorps, which included two Luftwaffe *Feld-Divisionen* (Field Divisions). A large amount of armour from the 11th and 20th Tank corps and 4th Guards Mechanised Corps nearly smashed Hollidt's left flank, but the rapid transfer of the veteran 17.Panzer-Division to this sector prevented a breakthrough. Over 180 of Tolbukhin's tanks were knocked out in five days of heavy fighting and his troops gained virtually no ground; Hollidt's last remaining reserves of manpower, fuel and ammunition, however, were nearly exhausted.

Throughout September, von Manstein could do little more than react to Soviet offensive jabs. The one exception was the Bukrin bridgehead, which Hoth hoped to crush with a strong counter-attack. However, Nehring's XXIV Panzerkorps only had part of 19.Panzer-Division and part of 57.Infanterie-Division containing the bridgehead, so Hoth deferred the counter-attack until elements of 7.Panzer-Division and 20.Panzergrenadier-Division could be deployed to this sector. Instead, the Germans contented themselves with shelling and bombing Vatutin's bridgeheads. Nevertheless, Vatutin used the respite wisely to push additional forces across the Dnepr and to fortify the existing bridgeheads. The first Soviet pontoon engineers reached the Dnepr on 26 September and they began ferrying some tanks and artillery across the river to Moskalenko's and Rybalko's armies. Just as the German reinforcements arrived in sector, Hoth decided to put von Knobelsdorff's XXXXVIII Panzerkorps in charge of the counter-attack, rather than Nehring's XXIV Panzerkorps; switching command and staff at this point was a poor tactical decision. When the Germans began their counter-attack on 29 September, they were not only shocked to encounter dug-in Soviet tanks and anti-tank guns, but quickly realised that the enemy greatly outnumbered them. Vatutin had crammed elements of 19 rifle divisions into the small Bukrin bridgehead. Von Knobelsdorff managed to inflict 2,800 casualties upon the troops in the bridgehead but soon decided to shift to the

An 8cm mortar crew from 217. Infanterie-Division prepares to shell one of the Soviet bridgeheads. Lacking sufficient infantry to crush the Soviet bridgeheads north of Kiev, the Germans were content to keep them under regular bombardment. (HITM)

defensive to conserve his own forces. The VIII Fliegerkorps succeeded in destroying one of the Soviet pontoon bridges across the Dnepr, but this was quickly rebuilt. Soviet engineers began building an underwater bridge across the Dnepr, just below the water's surface, that was difficult to spot from the air. On 30 September, the Soviets counter-attacked with 300 tanks from Rybalko's 3rd Guards Tank Army and four rifle divisions from the 40th Army, but failed to gain any ground.

While the Germans were focused on crushing the Bukrin bridgehead, Vatutin continued to try and gain a bridgehead north of Kiev. On 28/29 September, General-major Nikandr E. Chibisov's 38th Army succeeded in establishing four small lodgements with the 51st Rifle Corps near Lyutezh, 25km north of Kiev. The German XIII Armeekorps had 82. and 208. Infanterie divisions in this sector, which were forced to cover a very wide front. The 82.Infanterie-Division managed to contain Chibisov's main effort south of Lyutezh, but the 51st Rifle Corps was able to gain a substantial lodgement in the marshy terrain east of Lyutezh. On 29 and 30 September, Chibisov began expanding his bridgehead but German resistance increased and the 51st Rifle Corps was limited to a lodgement that was only 1km deep. Given the wild, marshy nature of the terrain in this sector, which had very few roads, Hoth was not overly concerned about this Soviet bridgehead.

By the end of September, Hoth's 4.Panzerarmee had abandoned its bridgehead on the east bank of the Dnepr near Kiev, defended by VIII Armeekorps, withdrawing the last of its troops to the west bank. Von Manstein slightly reconfigured his army boundaries, giving Wöhler's 8.Armee responsibility for containing the Bukrin bridgehead, so Hoth could focus on

An SdKfz 250 light half-track from one of the Panzer divisions' reconnaissance battalions, which served as highly mobile reaction forces to contest Soviet crossings over the Dnepr. Since initially the Soviets had few anti-tank guns in their forward units, even lightly armoured vehicles proved to be a real threat to the ad hoc bridgeheads. (Author's collection)

The Soviets used the cover of night to move additional troops into their bridgeheads over the Dnepr. The Germans harassed the crossing sites with artillery, but could not stop the flow of troops across the river. (Author's collection)

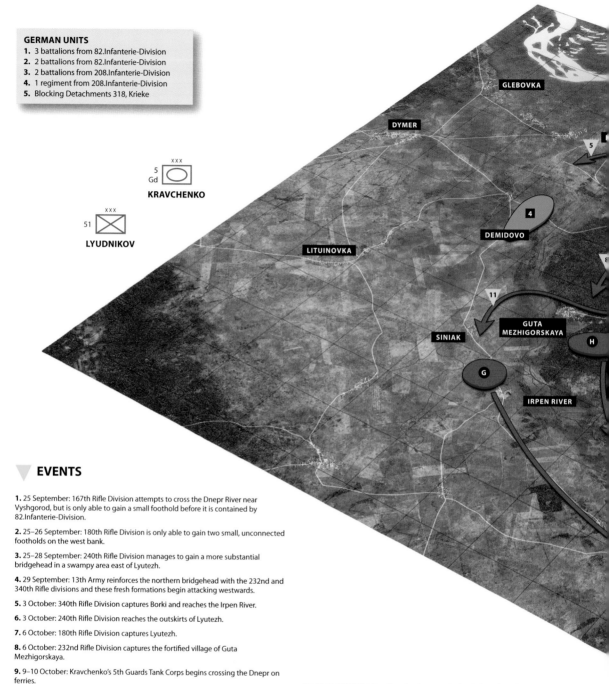

GERMAN UNITS

1. 3 battalions from 82.Infanterie-Division
2. 2 battalions from 82.Infanterie-Division
3. 2 battalions from 208.Infanterie-Division
4. 1 regiment from 208.Infanterie-Division
5. Blocking Detachments 318, Krieke

GLEBOVKA

DYMER

5
Gd xxx
KRAVCHENKO

51 xxx
LYUDNIKOV

LITUINOVKA

DEMIDOVO

4

11

GUTA
MEZHIGORSKAYA

SINIAK

G

H

IRPEN RIVER

▼ EVENTS

1. 25 September: 167th Rifle Division attempts to cross the Dnepr River near Vyshgorod, but is only able to gain a small foothold before it is contained by 82.Infanterie-Division.

2. 25–26 September: 180th Rifle Division is only able to gain two small, unconnected footholds on the west bank.

3. 25–28 September: 240th Rifle Division manages to gain a more substantial bridgehead in a swampy area east of Lyutezh.

4. 29 September: 13th Army reinforces the northern bridgehead with the 232nd and 340th Rifle divisions and these fresh formations begin attacking westwards.

5. 3 October: 340th Rifle Division captures Borki and reaches the Irpen River.

6. 3 October: 240th Rifle Division reaches the outskirts of Lyutezh.

7. 6 October: 180th Rifle Division captures Lyutezh.

8. 6 October: 232nd Rifle Division captures the fortified village of Guta Mezhigorskaya.

9. 9–10 October: Kravchenko's 5th Guards Tank Corps begins crossing the Dnepr on ferries.

10. Night 10/11 October: 5th Guards Tank Corps assembles in a wooded area west of Lyutezh.

11. 11 October: the breakout battle begins at 1200hrs and the 6th Guards Motorised Rifle Brigade captures a German bridge over the Irpen, then seizes Siniak by dusk.

12. Night, 11/12 October: Kravchenko commits the 20th and 22nd Guards Tank brigades over the Irpen to widen the breach. They succeed in capturing Gostomel and nearly reach the Kiev–Korosten rail line.

13. 12 October: two German blocking detachments are hastily shifted to prevent further exploitation by the 5th Guards Tank Corps.

CREATION OF THE LYUTEZH BRIDGEHEAD, 25 SEPTEMBER–12 OCTOBER 1943

The Soviet 51st Rifle Corps from Pukhov's 13th Army began crossing the Dnepr River in the Lyutezh sector. Opposing them, elements of two German infantry divisions from XIII Armeekorps fought a lopsided battle for over two weeks in a desperate effort to contain the Soviet bridgehead.

Note: Gridlines are shown at intervals of 2km (1.24 miles)

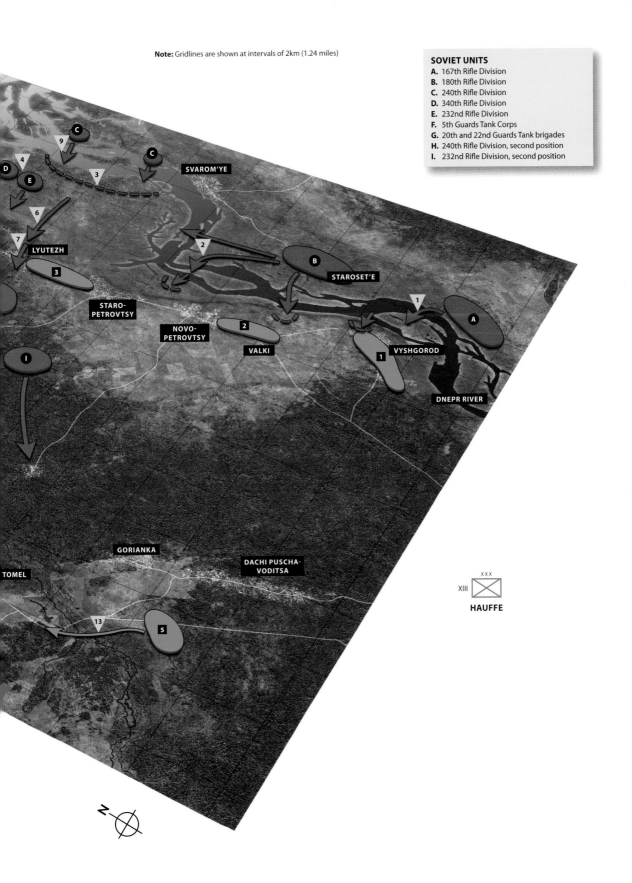

SOVIET UNITS
A. 167th Rifle Division
B. 180th Rifle Division
C. 240th Rifle Division
D. 340th Rifle Division
E. 232nd Rifle Division
F. 5th Guards Tank Corps
G. 20th and 22nd Guards Tank brigades
H. 240th Rifle Division, second position
I. 232nd Rifle Division, second position

SVAROM'YE

STAROSET'E

LYUTEZH

STARO-
PETROVTSY

NOVO-
PETROVTSY

VALKI

VYSHGOROD

DNEPR RIVER

GORIANKA

DACHI PUSCHA-
VODITSA

TOMEL

XXX
XIII

HAUFFE

A Soviet Maxim machine-gun crew on the banks of the Dnepr. The rapid Soviet build-up in the Bukrin bridgehead shocked the Germans, but the mass of forces Vatutin assembled in it never actually succeeded in breaking out of their entrenched stronghold.

the bridgeheads north of Kiev. From von Manstein's point of view in his headquarters at Kirovograd, the situation was serious along most of his 700km-long front, but no longer critical. While Rokossovsky, Vatutin and Konev had all gained minor bridgeheads across the Dnepr, they were more or less contained and von Manstein knew that the OKH was dispatching strong reinforcements to Heeresgruppe Süd. With any luck, the reinforcements would allow von Manstein to crush these bridgeheads and establish a stable front behind the Dnepr. From the Soviet point of view, the Dnepr had already been compromised as a barrier and the only troubling factor was that logistical problems delayed the construction of pontoon bridges, which restricted to a trickle the transfer of artillery and tanks to the west bank. Yet once these deficiencies were corrected, Stavka was confident that the main strength of the Red Army could be employed to break out of the Dnepr bridgeheads and advance to crush Heeresgruppe Süd.

OCTOBER: BATTLE FOR THE BRIDGEHEADS

Once the initial bridgeheads were established, Stavka directed Rokossovsky, Vatutin and Konev to prepare plans to break out of them in early October, but this proved to be far more difficult to execute than it appeared to planners in Moscow. Rokossovsky's forces were in the best position to affect a break out, since Pukhov's 13th Army had cleared out a large area on the west side of the Dnepr and could cooperate with the 60th and 61st armies on its flanks. Pukhov was already attacking southwards and on 1 October, troops from his 15th Rifle Corps liberated Chernobyl and forced 8.Panzer-Division to retreat. However, General der Infanterie Kurt von der Chevallerie's LIX Armeekorps was able to establish a strong defensive line just south of the

Pripiat River which prevented both Pukhov's 13th Army and Cherniakhovsky's 60th Army from advancing southwards towards Kiev. Furthermore, *Kampfgruppen* from the 2., 4., 5. and 7. Panzer divisions arrived to mount a counter-attack which recaptured Chernobyl on 4 October. Although all the German units were relatively small, they were mobile and Pukhov's 13th Army found itself overextended. A series of German pincer attacks gradually surrounded the 15th Rifle Corps and also forced the 60th Army to fall back to the Dnepr. After a week of fighting, the 15th Rifle Corps was demolished and

Soviet troops who crossed the Dnepr north of Kiev had to contend with the marshy terrain adjoining the Pripet Marshes, which inhibited their ability to advance westwards. Von Manstein regarded this area as a secondary concern, since he believed that the Soviets would not be able to employ large armoured units in this sector. (Courtesy of the Central Museum of the Armed Forces, Moscow via Stavka)

about 3,000 survivors retreated into the swamps to link up with local partisans. The successful German counter-attack had neutralised the Soviet bridgeheads in this sector for the time being and Stavka decided to transfer the 13th and 60th armies to Vatutin's front to improve command and control.

Vatutin's forces in the Lyutezh and Bukrin bridgeheads lacked the fuel and ammunition to mount a major breakout effort for some time and, instead, were forced to slowly expand their lodgements against increasing German resistance. Chibisov's 38th Army managed to reach the Irpen River by 3 October but was soon blocked by XIII Armeekorps' 82. and 208.Infanterie divisions. Vatutin provided Chibisov with General-major Andrei G. Kravchenko's 5th Guards Tank Corps to expand his bridgehead, but lack of pontoon bridging assets delayed the commitment of armour into the Lyutezh bridgehead. Kravchenko was able to get about 90 of his tanks (50 T-34s, 15 Churchills and 25 T-70s) across the Desna River on 4/5 October by fording

German infantry in entrenchments in a wooded area, with plenty of grenades at the ready. This Landser appears to have pinned photos of his family and girlfriend to the nearby tree, which is likely to distract him from watching for the threat to his front. Note the captured Soviet grenade at the base of the tree. (Nik Cornish at www.Stavka.org.uk)

The Soviet breakout from the Myshuryn Rog bridgehead, 15–25 October 1943.

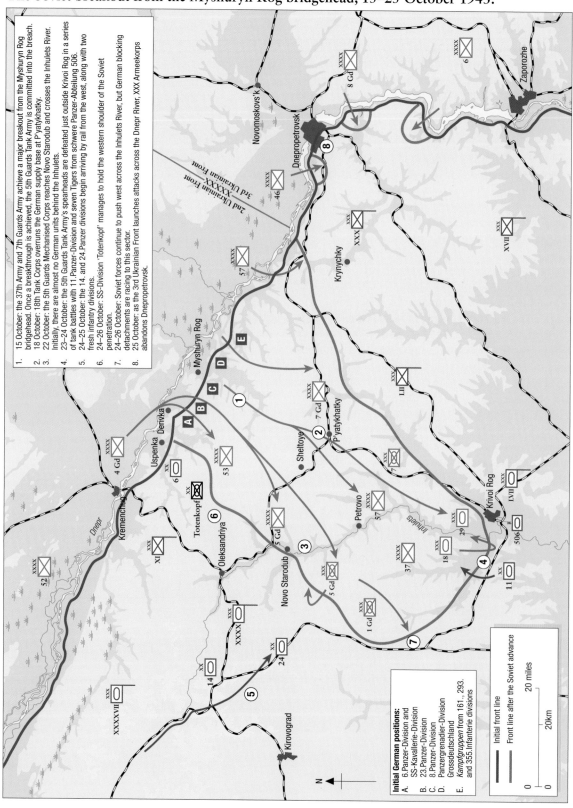

1. 15 October: the 37th Army and 7th Guards Army achieve a major breakout from the Myshuryn Rog bridgehead. Once a breakthrough is achieved, the 5th Guards Tank Army is committed into the breach.
2. 18 October: 18th Tank Corps overruns the German supply base at P'yatykhatky.
3. 22 October: the 5th Guards Mechanised Corps reaches Novo Starodub and crosses the Inhulets River. Initially, there are almost no German units behind the Inhulets.
4. 23–24 October: the 5th Guards Tank Army's spearheads are defeated just outside Krivoi Rog in a series of tank battles with 11.Panzer-Division and seven Tigers from schwere Panzer-Abteilung 506.
5. 24–25 October: the 14. and 24.Panzer divisions begin arriving by rail from the west, along with two fresh infantry divisions.
6. 24–26 October: SS-Division 'Totenkopf' manages to hold the western shoulder of the Soviet penetration.
7. 24–26 October: Soviet forces continue to push west across the Inhulets River, but German blocking detachments are racing to this sector.
8. 25 October: as the 3rd Ukrainian Front launches attacks across the Dnepr River, XXX Armeekorps abandons Dnepropetrovsk.

Initial German positions:
A. 6.Panzer-Division and SS-Kavallerie-Division
B. 23.Panzer-Division
C. 8.Panzer-Division
D. Panzergrenadier-Division Grossdeutschland
E. *Kampfgruppen* from 161., 293. and 355.Infanterie divisions

Initial front line
Front line after the Soviet advance

20 miles

20km

at a spot where the river was narrow and only 1–2m deep, but had to wait until 9 October for Soviet engineers to establish a DMP-42 ferry site across the Dnepr at Svarom'e. Although German artillery repeatedly shelled the ferry site, all of Kravchenko's tanks were finally across the Dnepr and in the Lyutezh bridgehead by the evening of 11 October.

As his forces west of the Dnepr increased, Vatutin intended to mount a coordinated breakout operation from the 60th Army's bridgeheads, as well as the Lyutezh and Bukrin bridgeheads in the second week of October. With only a handful of pontoon bridges constructed, Soviet supplies of fuel and ammunition in the bridgeheads was minimal, but Vatutin wanted to attack before Hoth could either crush any of the bridgeheads or receive significant reinforcements. Cherniakhovsky's 60th Army attacked first, on 9–10 October, from its bridgehead near Gornostaipol'. Massing several rifle divisions and a tank regiment south of the Teterev River, Cherniakhovsky achieved a breakthrough in the sector held by the German 183.Infanterie-Division and then pushed General-leytenant Viktor K. Baranov's 1st Guards Cavalry Corps into the breach. The Soviet cavalry were able to penetrate 15km into the German front, but the timely arrival of *Kampfgruppen* from the 7. and 8.Panzer divisions sealed off the penetration after several days of fighting.

Chibisov's 38th Army attacked on the morning of 11 October and mechanised rifle troops were able to capture an intact bridge across the Irpen River at Siniak, but the German 82. and 208.Infanterie divisions managed to retain control over the towns of Demidovo and Lyutezh on the shoulders of the Soviet penetration. Kravchenko's tanks were set to exploit into the void across the Irpen River, but Chibisov was worried about his flanks. Hoth sent his only reserve in this sector – 68.Infanterie-Division – to reinforce the wavering XIII Armeekorps and ordered the Luftwaffe to destroy the bridge at Siniak. On the morning of 12 October, German bombers damaged the Siniak bridge; Soviet sappers lacked the resources to repair it. Chibisov opted to redirect his main effort southwards, to eliminate 82.Infanterie-Division's strongpoint at Lyutezh. After four days of heavy pounding, Chibisov's infantry and Kravchenko's tanks finally forced the XIII Armeekorps to abandon Lyutezh and the Soviets gained 8km. However, the 13th, 38th and 60th armies were temporarily fought out and could not continue offensive operations,

Soviet sappers search for mines along a river-crossing site. German security troops had mined some crossing sites and emplaced barbed-wire obstacles to inhibit the movement of Soviet partisans, but these proved little hindrance to the Red Army. (Author's collection)

A Panther being towed by two Zugkraftwagen 18t (SdKfz 9), in September 1943. The Panther continued to be bedevilled with technical malfunctions, which undermined the German intention of using it to regain armoured supremacy on the Eastern Front. Instead, the Panther had a very low operational readiness rate and dozens were abandoned and blown up by their crews. (Bundesarchiv Bild 101I-240-2145-15; photo: Casper)

despite bullying efforts by Georgy Zhukov (in his role as Stavka representative) to keep the pressure on the Germans. These three Soviet armies suffered over 85,000 casualties in October, or roughly one-third of their strength.

In the Bukrin sector, the Germans launched a surprise counter-attack on 1 October with SS-Panzergrenadier-Division 'Das Reich' against the Grebeni bridgehead, west of Rzhyshchiv. This small bridgehead was held by the 52nd Rifle Corps from Moskalenko's 40th Army, but was not connected to the rest of the Bukrin–Rzhyshchiv bridgeheads. 'Das Reich' had no operational tanks, but instead attacked with four Panzergrenadier battalions, its reconnaissance battalion and a few assault guns. After four days of heavy fighting, the isolated Grebeni bridgehead was overrun. Although Vatutin's forces made several small efforts to expand the Bukrin bridgehead in early October, Vatutin succeeded in convincing Zhukov of the need to build up resources for a proper set-piece offensive. In the interim, reinforcements poured into the bridgeheads, including the 10th Tank Corps and 8th Guards Tank Corps

A German howitzer shells the Soviet bridgeheads. The retreat to the Dnepr cost Heeresgruppe Süd a fair amount of its artillery, which further reduced German defensive capabilities. Unlike the Soviets, who were about to conduct lengthy artillery preparations with hundreds of guns, the German artillery was reduced to a harassing role. (HITM)

and infantry from the 27th Army. The 47th Army also succeeded in establishing a small bridgehead across the Dnepr at Studenets just north of Kanev. By the second week of October, Vatutin had about 680 tanks and self-propelled guns and 14 rifle divisions in the bridgehead, opposing seven German divisions with about 150 tanks. Yet at this point, the Bukrin, Rzhyshchiv and Studenets bridgeheads were still not connected, which made it difficult for Vatutin to coordinate actions of the 40th and 47th armies and 3rd Guards Tank Army. Vatutin prepared to launch his set-piece breakout offensive on 12 October.

However, Wöhler had no intention of allowing Vatutin to simply amass an overwhelming force on the west bank. By early October he received 3. Panzer-Division and additional infantry for the Bukrin sector and he deployed XXIV Panzerkorps to contain the Rzhyshchiv bridgehead, XXXXVIII Panzerkorps to contain Bukrin and III Panzerkorps to encircle the Studenets bridgehead. German pioneers laid anti-tank minefields along likely enemy avenues of approach and German artillery kept the bridgeheads under constant fire. Having crushed the Grebeni bridgehead, 'Das Reich' launched a spoiling attack against 40th Army's Rzhyshchiv bridgehead on 10 October that drove the Soviets back 1km.

At 0700hrs on 12 October, Vatutin's artillery began a 40-minute artillery preparation and then a total of 15 rifle divisions launched simultaneous attacks from the Rzhyshchiv, Bukrin and Studenets bridgeheads. Most of Rybalko's 3rd Guards Tank Army was massed in the eastern side of the Bukrin bridgehead, weighting the effort in that sector. Although the Soviet infantry, supported by tanks, was able to gain several kilometres of terrain, the effort to link up the three bridgeheads failed. Zhukov ordered Vatutin to

A German armoured *Kampfgruppe* from 24.Panzer-Division forming up in an assembly area for a counter-attack with Panzergrenadiers in SPW half-tracks, supported by self-propelled 2cm flak guns and Marder tank destroyers. The German Panzer divisions relied upon a combined-arms mix of forces to create their combat power. Relatively few tanks were operational in the early stages of the Dnepr campaign. The *Kampfgruppe* from 19.Panzer-Division that defeated the Kanev airborne landings had a composition similar to this. (HITM)

ROTMISTROV'S TANKERS EXACT REVENGE FOR PROKHOROVKA, 18 OCTOBER 1943 (PP. 60–61)

Battlefield atrocities were commonly committed by both sides on the Eastern Front, but they still remain something of a taboo subject. The defeated have no wish to recount their misdeeds and the victors have tried to bury all recollection of their own crimes. On 15 October 1943, Konev's forces began a massive offensive to break out from the Myshuryn Rog bridgehead, spearheaded by Rotmistrov's 5th Guards Tank Army. Within two days, the Soviet 7th Guards Army broke through LVII Panzerkorps' front and Rotmistrov's armour surged southwards in pursuit. Rotmistrov's 5th Guards Tank Army had suffered near-crippling losses at the hands of Hoth's 4.Panzerarmee at the battle of Prokhorovka in July and then again at Bogodukhov in August, which were both tactical defeats. However, Rotmistrov's 5th Guards Tank Army had since been rebuilt and its veteran tankers pursued the fleeing German troops with great zeal. On the evening of 18 October, Rotmistrov's tankers approached the important rail junction of P'yatykhatky, 45km south of Myshuryn Rog, and found the opportunity had arrived for revenge against the hated invaders.

Although 23.Panzer-Division tried to make a stand at P'yatykhatky, Rotmistrov's tankers arrived too soon. German rear echelon troops in the town panicked and fled in a massive column, which the Soviets shelled mercilessly. Soviet T-34s (**1**), with infantry desant troops mounted on their back decks, drove straight to the train station and captured a train loaded with ten brand-new Tiger I tanks (**2**), destined for Panzergrenadier-Division 'Grossdeutschland'. Another train (**3**) in the station was discovered loaded with wounded German troops. The Soviet infantrymen (**4**) tossed hand grenades through the train windows and then finished off others with their submachine guns. The tide had turned – now the Wehrmacht was running and being slaughtered – and the Red Army intended to keep it that way all the way to Berlin.

continue attacking for three more days, which only resulted in heavy casualties but no significant gains. Shortages of heavy artillery ammunition (particularly 122mm and 152mm) severely impacted Vatutin's ability to fight a protracted battle against a dug-in enemy. German anti-tank defences also exacted a heavy price in Soviet tanks knocked out, including 107 from the 6th Guards Tank Corps. After incessant badgering from Zhukov, Vatutin shifted Rybalko's 3rd Guards Tank Army to the western side of the Bukrin bridgehead and attempted to break through to the 40th Army's Rzhyshchiv bridgehead on 21 October. A massed assault with infantry, tanks and artillery was only able to advance 1km before it was literally shot to pieces by German artillery and anti-tank guns. Vatutin was stunned to discover that 'Das Reich' had constructed two strong lines of defence, fronted by mines, which could not be broken. Even the Luftwaffe made an appearance over the battlefield, further disrupting the Soviet attack. Rybalko lost 65 per cent of his remaining armour in a single day, which forced Vatutin to abort the offensive. Altogether, Vatutin's forces in the Bukrin sector suffered 27,938 casualties in these two offensives. Against improbable odds, Wöhler's defence at Bukrin had held and Vatutin was now left with a large percentage of his forces crammed into three small, unconnected and almost useless bridgeheads.

In contrast to Vatutin's difficulties, Konev's Steppe Front had slightly better logistical support and was able to construct a pontoon bridge over the Dnepr near Borodaivka by 2 October, which enabled tanks to cross. Once resupplied and supported by tanks, the 7th Guards Army was able to push out of its tiny bridgeheads and capture Myshuryn Rog. Generalleutnant Nikolaus von Vormann's 23.Panzer-Division mounted a puny counter-attack with a company of pioneers and seven tanks, but could not stop Konev's advance. Recognising the potential of this sector, on 3 October Stavka transferred Rotmistrov's 5th Guards Tank Army to Konev's command; Rotmistrov's tank army was badly blooded at Kursk but had just spent three weeks rebuilding and was ready to return to battle. Using great stealth, Rotmistrov began moving his tank army 200km forward to the Dnepr in a series of night marches, which Luftwaffe aerial reconnaissance failed to detect.

Konev's Myshuryn Rog lodgement was near the boundary of Wöhler's 8.Armee and von Mackensen's 1. Panzerarmee, but the main defence comprised the latter's LII Armeekorps, with *Kampfgruppen* from the 62. and

An SU-76M self-propelled in an overrun German position. Soviet efforts to break out of the Bukrin bridgehead resulted in a serious of brutal battles, with heavy losses on both sides. (From the fonds of the RGAKFD in Krasnogorsk via Stavka)

306.Infanterie divisions. With 23.Panzer-Division unable to contain Konev's forces, Mackensen sent the elite 'Grossdeutschland' division to try and stabilise this sector. However, 'Grossdeutschland' had only 15 operational tanks, including five Tigers. Von Mackensen was forced to spread out his depleted armoured units to cover too wide an area, which meant that the German infantry could expect little more than a platoon or two of tanks to support even the most critical sectors.

Despite the limited forces available, von Mackensen knew that he had to crush the Myshuryn Rog lodgement before it grew any larger. Kirchner's LVII Panzerkorps was brought up and both 23.Panzer-Division and 'Grossdeutschland' were subordinated to this command and received priority for replacements and spare parts. By 8 October, Kirchner had assembled about 35–40 tanks and decided to attack the eastern end of the Soviet bridgehead in order to threaten one of the pontoon bridges. The initial attack by Vormann's 23.Panzer-Division achieved minor tactical success, but 'Grossdeutschland' delayed its attack for another 24 hours and ran into an alert enemy. A group of five Tiger Is advancing without adequate infantry support was surrounded and all five tanks were first immobilised, then destroyed by anti-tank guns. After this debacle, Kirchner called off his counter-attack, which enabled Rotmistrov to begin moving part of the 5th Guards Tank Army into the Myshuryn Rog lodgement.

Konev patiently assembled an overwhelming force on the west bank, consisting of the 37th Army and 7th Guards Army, then attacked on the morning of 15 October. After a massive artillery preparation, seven Soviet divisions punched through the thin perimeter held by 23.Panzer-Division, and then 7th Mechanised Corps and part of 18th Tank Corps were committed in the second wave of the attack. Vormann's 23.Panzer-Division mounted a hasty counter-attack but lost three of its eight remaining tanks, then fell back. The next day, Rotmistrov committed all of 5th Guards Tank Army into the offensive and gained more ground, creating a 10km-wide dent in the German

A Lend-Lease Valentine tank heads down to a crossing site over the Dnepr. The Red Army received over 3,000 Valentines during World War II and they were well liked in the infantry support role. The Red Army also used Churchill and Sherman tanks in the Dnepr campaign. (From the fonds of the RGAKFD in Krasnogorsk via Stavka)

front. Soviet tanks pushed into the gap, first overrunning 23.Panzer-Division's Flak-Bataillon, then attacking the divisional command post of 'Grossdeutschland'. In a futile effort, 23.Panzer-Division tried to block Rotmistrov's advance with just six tanks, but by 17 October Konev had achieved a major breakthrough. Rotmistrov's armour advanced at rapid pace to the south and south-west, overrunning German support units and continuing to advance even during the night. Kirchner's entire LVII Panzerkorps was forced to retreat in haste, which caused problems for German command and control.

At the important rail junction of P'yatykhatky, 45km south of Myshuryn Rog, Vormann's 23.Panzer-Division tried to make a stand but Rotmistrov's tankers overran the town on the evening of 18 October. Ten brand-new Tiger I tanks, destined for 'Grossdeutschland', were captured intact on rail cars in the train station. Rotmistrov's tankers also shot up a massive German column, consisting of over 3,000 vehicles, that was attempting to escape the south side of the town. Vormann's threadbare 23.Panzer-Division was too weak to interfere and was forced to retreat or be destroyed. In a matter of just three days, Konev had driven a huge wedge between 8.Armee and 1. Panzerarmee and was presented with a golden opportunity to unhinge the entire German defence along the Dnepr. Konev was faced with the kind of choice that can decide a campaign: advance west to Kirovograd to roll up 8.Armee's right flank or advance south to Krivoi Rog to outflank 1. Panzerarmee. Yet rather than choose one course of action and commit his main effort to achieving it, Konev decided to split his forces and attempt to capture both objectives. He sent the 53rd Army and the 5th Guards Mechanised Corps towards Kirovograd and the 18th and 29th Tank corps to Krivoi Rog. For a few days, German resistance was negligible as units retreated out of the way of Rotmistrov's tankers and the 5th Guards Mechanised Corps reached Novo Starodub on the Inhulets River on 22 October. Rotmistrov's push to the south also caused von Mackensen to

A column of German Panther tanks, apparently damaged and abandoned in a Ukrainian village. During the counter-attacks in November 1943, German armoured units were hindered by fuel and spare-part shortages, which often left units immobilised. These tanks were probably disabled by their own crews. (Nik Cornish at www.Stavka.org.uk)

abandon Dnepropetrovsk on 25 October, in fear of his lines of communications being cut. Two days later, the vanguard of 5th Guards Tank Army reached the outskirts of Krivoi Rog. Malinovsky's South-Western Front (redesignated 3rd Ukrainian Front on 20 October) had not yet secured a bridgehead across the Dnepr but von Mackensen's retreat allowed it to surge across the river with the 46th Army and 8th Guards Army.

Then – as often happened in Soviet mobile operations – entropy set in and Rotmistrov's offensive began to run out of steam. Rotmistrov's forward tank brigades ran out of fuel and Soviet logistical units had not been prioritised in getting across the Dnepr. Rotmistrov also found it difficult to coordinate an army that had been split along two diverging axes – a clear violation of the military principle of unity of effort. Von Manstein also began to receive powerful reinforcements from the West: 14. and 24.Panzer divisions, each equipped with 49 PzKpfw IV tanks and 44 StuG III assault guns. These two divisions had been destroyed at Stalingrad eight months before, but had been rebuilt from surviving cadre and fresh recruits. As the trains carrying these two divisions began arriving in the Ukraine, von Manstein ordered them to unload near Wöhler's 8.Armee headquarters in Kirovograd. Von Manstein

Soviet infantry in urban combat. Red Army weapons and tactics were well suited to close-quarters fighting. (Author's collection)

also transferred the XXXX Panzerkorps staff and Major Willing's Tiger battalion from the Zaporozhe bridgehead and shifted 11.Panzer-Division and SS-Panzergrenadier-Division 'Totenkopf' to assemble for a counter-offensive against Rotmistrov's 5th Guards Tank Army. Von Manstein intended to use these formations to conduct another 'Backhand Blow'-type counter-offensive, like the one that had wrecked Rybalko's 3rd Tank Army in March 1943.

Yet just as von Manstein's counter-offensive was beginning to take shape, Hitler decided to interfere. He ordered that General der Gebirgstruppe Ferdinand Schörner, currently stationed in Finland, be flown in to take command of XXXX Panzerkorps and lead the operation. Schörner was completely unfamiliar with the situation in the Ukraine and had no experience with mechanised operations, but he was an ardent Nazi and a ruthless commander – both factors which Hitler found attractive. When Schörner arrived, he imprudently decided to accelerate the operational timetable, even though parts of 14. and 24.Panzer divisions were still en route. He also decided to modify von Manstein's plan by attacking the face of the Soviet salient, instead of its base, relying on brute force rather than the pincer tactics favoured by the Panzer divisions.

On 28 October, Schörner's counter-offensive began with SS-Panzergrenadier-Division 'Totenkopf' attacking the 5th Guards Mechanised Corps and 11.Panzer-Division attacking Rotmistrov's stalled vanguard near Krivoi Rog. Rotmistrov's right flank was wide open, because infantry from the 37th Army had not yet arrived to cover this sector. Elements of 14. and 24.Panzer divisions joined the counter-offensive on 29 October, pushing straight into the gap. Rotmistrov was stunned by the German counter-offensive and was forced to fall back from Krivoi Rog, but none of his units were cut off and destroyed. Instead, Schörner's counter-offensive succeeded in plugging the gap between 8.Armee and 1.Panzerarmee and disrupting Stavka's timetable. Von Manstein recognised that a great opportunity had been lost to smash Rotmistrov's 5th Guards Tank Army, but he lacked the moral courage to stand up to Hitler or Schörner and instead allowed their interference to undermine Heeresgruppe Süd's performance. Just as Schörner's counter-offensive was concluding, two fresh units – 1.Panzer-Division and 1.SS-Panzer-Division Leibstandarte SS Adolf Hitler – were arriving in Kirovograd and von Manstein hoped to use them in a follow-up offensive against Konev's forces.

While Malinovsky's South-Western Front had been unable to cross the Dnepr without help from Konev's forces, it had put paid to the Zaporozhe bridgehead. The XXXX Panzerkorps was able to hold off the 3rd and 8th Guards armies for the first two weeks of October, thanks to Major Willing's Tigers schwere Panzer-Abteilung 506 and Major Georg Baumunk's Ferdinands. However, German losses were heavy and Heinrici, the XXXX Panzerkorps commander, was severely wounded. Malinovsky made repeated assaults upon XXXX Panzerkorps' positions, including armour from the 23rd Tank Corps and 1st Guards Mechanised Corps, but all attacks were repulsed. In one particularly strong attack on 10 October, the Germans claimed 48 enemy tanks knocked out. Yet Heeresgruppe Süd was in no position to win a battle of attrition and Malinovsky played the Red Army's trump card – artillery.

A German StuG III assault gun receives ammunition replenishment. The StuG III was an excellent defensive weapon with its low silhouette and thick frontal armour, but it was less useful as a tank substitute in mobile operations. (Nik Cornish at www.Stavka.org.uk)

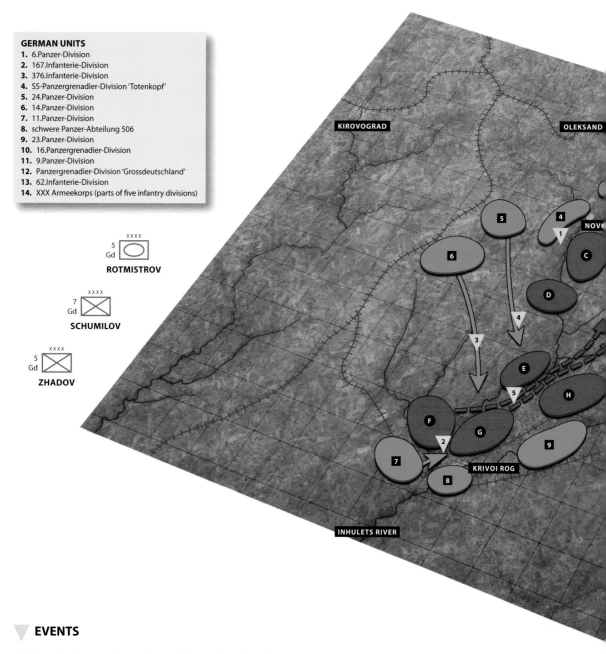

GERMAN UNITS

1. 6.Panzer-Division
2. 167.Infanterie-Division
3. 376.Infanterie-Division
4. SS-Panzergrenadier-Division 'Totenkopf'
5. 24.Panzer-Division
6. 14.Panzer-Division
7. 11.Panzer-Division
8. schwere Panzer-Abteilung 506
9. 23.Panzer-Division
10. 16.Panzergrenadier-Division
11. 9.Panzer-Division
12. Panzergrenadier-Division 'Grossdeutschland'
13. 62.Infanterie-Division
14. XXX Armeekorps (parts of five infantry divisions)

ROTMISTROV

SCHUMILOV

ZHADOV

▼ EVENTS

1. 28 October: the German counter-attack begins with 'Totenkopf' launching a fixing attack against the 5th Guards Mechanised Corps.

2. 28 October: 11.Panzer-Division also attacks to fix the 5th Guards Tank Army spearheads near Krivoi Rog.

3. 29 October: although incomplete, 14.Panzer-Division begins advancing into 5th Guards Tank Army's unprotected right flank.

4. 30 October: 24.Panzer-Division joins the offensive, caving in 5th Guards Tank Army's right flank. Faced with encirclement, the 18th and 29th Tank corps conduct a fighting retreat.

5. 31 October: Schörner's counter-attack conducts mop-up operations against the retreating Soviets, but no enemy units are destroyed. The Soviet salient is eliminated.

SCHÖRNER'S COUNTER-OFFENSIVE NEAR KRIVOI ROG, 28–31 OCTOBER 1943

As Konev's breakout from the Myshuryn Rog bridgehead ebbed and Rotmistrov's 5th Guards Tank Army was handicapped by logistical problems, substantial German reinforcements arrived from the West. Hitler ordered Schörner's XXXX Panzerkorps to seal the breach in the German front and destroy the Soviet armour with a traditional pincer attack, but the results fell short of expectations.

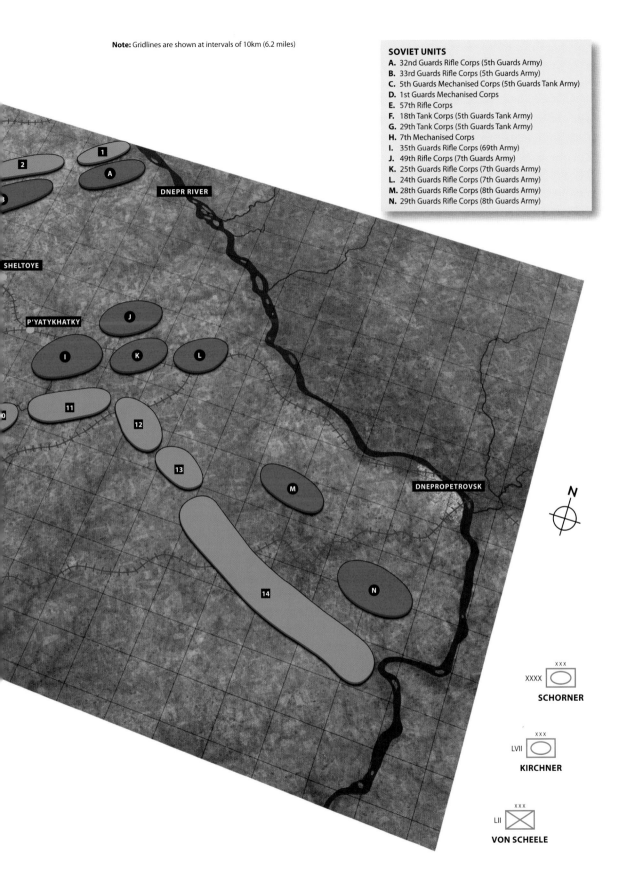

Note: Gridlines are shown at intervals of 10km (6.2 miles)

SOVIET UNITS
A. 32nd Guards Rifle Corps (5th Guards Army)
B. 33rd Guards Rifle Corps (5th Guards Army)
C. 5th Guards Mechanised Corps (5th Guards Tank Army)
D. 1st Guards Mechanised Corps
E. 57th Rifle Corps
F. 18th Tank Corps (5th Guards Tank Army)
G. 29th Tank Corps (5th Guards Tank Army)
H. 7th Mechanised Corps
I. 35th Guards Rifle Corps (69th Army)
J. 49th Rifle Corps (7th Guards Army)
K. 25th Guards Rifle Corps (7th Guards Army)
L. 24th Guards Rifle Corps (7th Guards Army)
M. 28th Guards Rifle Corps (8th Guards Army)
N. 29th Guards Rifle Corps (8th Guards Army)

DNEPR RIVER

SHELTOYE

P'YATYKHATKY

DNEPROPETROVSK

SCHORNER

KIRCHNER

VON SCHEELE

Malinovsky massed the 7th and 9th Artillery divisions against the Zaporozhe bridgehead and began smashing the German infantry positions. By mid-October, heavy losses had made the Zaporozhe bridgehead untenable and von Mackensen ordered Heinrici's XXXX Panzerkorps to evacuate the east bank. Seven Tigers had been destroyed in the bridgehead and two damaged ones abandoned, but the remainder of Major Willing's battalion was ferried across the Dnepr on pontoons. Then on the night of 14 October, German pioneers blew up the massive hydroelectric dam near Zaporozhe.

On the south end of the line, Hollidt's 6.Armee managed to maintain its grip on the Melitopol position for several weeks, despite a hard and constant pounding from Tolbukhin's Southern Front. On 10 October, Tolbukhin achieved a breakthrough in the vulnerable IV Armeekorps sector with the 20th Tank Corps and 4th Guards Mechanised Corps, but 13. Panzer-Division, reinforced with a fresh battalion of Panther tanks, counter-attacked and drove them back. Minor tactical victories like that left Hitler enthusiastic about using Melitopol as a springboard for a future offensive, even though it was clear to everyone else that this exposed position could not be held. Finally, on 23 October Hollidt abandoned Melitopol and began falling back towards Kherson on the Dnepr. Amazingly, Hitler allowed part of 6.Armee to withdraw behind the Dnepr, but he ordered IV and XXIX Armeekorps to retain a bridgehead on the east side of the river to defend the approaches to Nikopol. Thus Hitler chained eight divisions, including 9.Panzer-Division, to the defence of the Nikopol bridgehead, for the sake of keeping Soviet artillery out of range of the manganese ore mines on the west bank. Hitler regarded the mineral mines around Nikopol as a critical resource, but was indifferent to the sacrifices this would require 6.Armee to make. By the end of October, Heeresgruppe A still had a line of communications running to 17.Armee in the Crimea, but these forces would soon be isolated. Hitler's decisions condemned von Kleist's Heeresgruppe A to inevitable defeat, with two of five corps about to be isolated in the Crimea, two tied to the Nikopol bridgehead and only XXXXIV Armeekorps available for defensive tasks on the west bank of the Dnepr.

On 20 October, Stavka had decided to redesignate all of the fronts involved in the Lower Dnepr operation. Vatutin's Voronezh Front became the 1st Ukrainian Front, Konev's Steppe Front became the 2nd Ukrainian Front, Malinovsky's South-Western Front became the 3rd Ukrainian Front and Tolbukhin's Southern Front became the 4th Ukrainian Front.

NOVEMBER: LIBERATION

Zhukov had been keen to continue the effort to break out of the Bukrin bridgehead because he erroneously believed that the German defences were about to break. In fact, Wöhler's defence had been reinforced throughout October. On 24 October, Zhukov sent his bull-headed appreciation of the situation to Moscow and even had the temerity to ask for another tank army to reinforce the next offensive. However, more sober minds in Stavka realised that cramming more forces into the already crowded Bukrin bridgehead was not a recipe for success. Even Stalin had come to regard the lodgement at Bukrin as a dead end and was casting about for an alternative means to get to Kiev. Someone – it is not clear who – suggested that Vatutin should shift his main effort to the Lyutezh bridgehead, which was closer to Kiev and where the German defences were less robust. On 25 October, Stalin concurred with this recommendation, overruling Zhukov. That night, Vatutin ordered Rybalko to quietly transfer his entire 3rd Guards Tank Army from the Bukrin bridgehead to Lyutezh.

In order for the plan to work, it was imperative that the Germans not discover that Rybalko's tank army was moving north. Vatutin conducted an elaborate *maskirovka* operation, including radio deception and leaving non-operational tanks in Bukrin, in order to conceal Rybalko's transfer. The weather assisted Soviet plans, with a period of rain and fog degrading Luftwaffe reconnaissance efforts. It also proved logistically challenging to move Rybalko's tank army 150km north to Lyutezh; since there were only three pontoon bridges over the Dnepr, it took him three nights to move his army out of the Bukrin bridgehead, then two more days to move north and cross the Desna, then cross the Dnepr again. However, the operation was not detected by the Germans and by the morning of 2 November, Rybalko's entire 3rd Guards Tank Army was assembled in the Lyutezh bridgehead. In addition, Vatutin reinforced General-polkovnik Kirill S. Moskalenko's 38th Army (Moskalenko having replaced Chibisov on 27 October) in the bridgehead and provided him with the 7th Artillery Corps to support his breakout operation.

Hoth had four battered infantry divisions (68., 88., 323. and 388.) from XIII Armeekorps holding the southern perimeter around the Lyutezh bridgehead, which von Manstein regarded as adequate. Just in case, Hoth stationed Generalmajor Gottfried Frölich's 8.Panzer Division nearby in tactical reserve, although this badly depleted unit only had 610 Panzergrenadiers and 545 other combat troops, plus 14 tanks in its I./Panzer-Regiment 10 (including seven PzKpfw IV tanks with long-barelled 7.5cm guns). While short on troops, Frölich's unit did have 64 Schützenpanzerwagen (SPWs) and 828 trucks, which gave it good tactical mobility. Frölich formed two *Kampfgruppen* to serve as a quick reaction force for XIII Armeekorps. However, neither he nor Hoth had any idea that a Soviet tank army had entered the Lyutezh bridgehead.

Soviet attacks against the Zaporozhe and Nikopol bridgeheads, 25 September–25 November 1943.

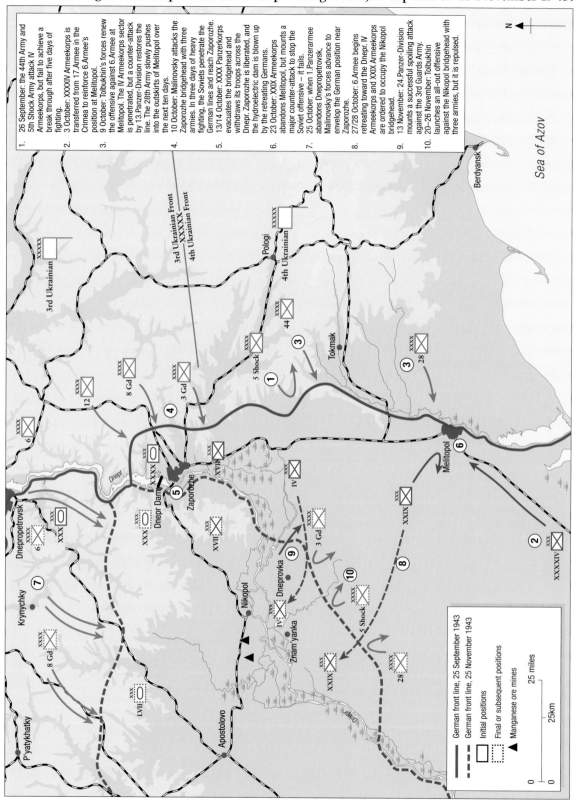

1. 26 September: the 44th Army and 5th Shock Army attack IV Armeekorps, but fail to achieve a break through after five days of fighting.

2. 3 October: XXXIV Armeekorps is transferred from 17.Armee in the Crimea to reinforce 6.Armee's position at Melitopol.

3. 9 October: Tolbukhin's forces renew the offensive against 6.Armee at Melitopol. The IV Armeekorps sector is penetrated, but a counter-attack by 13.Panzer-Division restores the line. The 28th Army slowly pushes into the outskirts of Melitopol over the next ten days.

4. 10 October: Malinovsky attacks the Zaporozhe bridgehead with three armies. In three days of heavy fighting, the Soviets penetrate the German lines and reach Zaporozhe.

5. 13/14 October: XXXX Panzerkorps evacuates the bridgehead and withdraws its troops across the Dnepr. Zaporozhe is liberated, and the hydroelectric dam is blown up by the retreating Germans.

6. 23 October: XXIX Armeekorps abandons Melitopol, but mounts a major counter-attack to stop the Soviet offensive – it fails.

7. 25 October: when 1.Panzerarmee abandons Dnepropetrovsk, Malinovsky's forces advance to envelop the German position near Zaporozhe.

8. 27/28 October: 6.Armee begins retreating toward the Dnepr. IV Armeekorps and XXIX Armeekorps are ordered to occupy the Nikopol bridgehead.

9. 13 November: 24.Panzer-Division mounts a successful spoiling attack against the 3rd Guards Army.

10. 20–26 November: Tolbukhin launches an all-out offensive against the Nikopol bridgehead with three armies, but it is repulsed.

Sea of Azov

German front line, 25 September 1943

German front line, 25 November 1943

Initial positions

Final or subsequent positions

Manganese ore mines

25 miles

25km

At 0800hrs on 3 November, Moskalenko's 38th Army started a 40-minute artillery preparation against the German positions opposite the south side of the Lyutezh bridgehead. The terrain held by XIII Armeekorps was a mix of farmland, wooded areas and marshes which was not favourable for the defence and the German units here had created a line of trenches but not the multi-layered defence that 8.Armee had constructed around the Bukrin bridgehead. The deluge of the 7th Artillery Corps' heavy artillery and Katyusha rockets crushed the forward German defences and left the survivors in a weakened condition to face the ground assault that commenced just after the artillery barrage lifted. Six rifle divisions from the 50th and 51st Rifle corps advanced southwards on line, followed by tanks from the 5th Guards Tank Corps. This time, Vatutin was able to employ proper combined-arms tactics and provided sapper teams to clear enemy mines and obstacles. The remaining German infantry and Panzerjäger fought desperately and managed to limit Moskalenko's initial attack to a 3km advance, but Moskalenko kept feeding in reserves and the 68. and 88.Infanterie divisions began to collapse. Frölich's 8.Panzer-Division was slow to react and then moved to support 208.Infanterie-Division near Siniak, even though it was not under heavy attack. Hoth hesitated to commit to 7.Panzer-Division, then sent it towards Irpen, rather than to mount a counter-attack to restore XIII Armeekorps' front. Seeing that the German defence was collapsing, Vatutin committed Rybalko's 3rd Guards Tank Army (6th Guards Tank Corps, 7th Guards Tank Corps and 9th Mechanised Corps) just before dusk and ordered him to continue attacking through the night. A large-scale tank attack at night over broken terrain was a highly unorthodox approach, but von Manstein certainly did not expect it. Indeed, von Manstein was still focused on Bukrin and believed that Hoth could contain the Soviet attack from Lyutezh within a few days.

While well suited to defensive combat, the Tiger was not invincible. This Tiger attempted to serve as a roadblock, but was apparently outflanked by more manoeuvrable T-34 tanks and its thinner rear armour penetrated. The poorly chosen position – in the middle of a road with no cover or concealment – suggests that the Tiger's crew was inexperienced. The proper employment in this situation is for the defending tank to occupy a hull-down position, making it more difficult to spot. (From the fonds of the RGAKFD in Krasnogorsk via Stavka)

Yet Hoth did not get a few days to react to Vatutin's offensive. Due to rainy weather on 4 November that blinded Luftwaffe aerial reconnaissance, Hoth still did not know that he was facing Rybalko's 3rd Guards Tank Army. He moved 7.Panzer-Division and 20.Panzergrenadier-Division to block the approaches to Kiev, anticipating that this would suffice to contain the 38th Army. Yet even before these units could arrive, Rybalko's rapid advance caused XIII Armeekorps to implode on 4 November and the 51st Rifle Corps and the 5th Guards Tanks Corps boldly pushed forward to the outskirts of Kiev. The 88.Infanterie-Division was virtually obliterated and the remnants of the rest of XIII Armeekorps retreated westwards towards Korosten. Rybalko's entire 3rd Guards Tank Army expertly pivoted to the south-west and advanced to sever the road and rail links into Kiev before the German tactical reserves could arrive. In another risky decision, Rybalko ordered his tankers to drive at night with their headlights on, which enabled the 7th Guards Tank Corps to reach the main road west of Kiev and then overwhelm the surprised blocking detachments from Frölich's 8.Panzer-Division. The Germans were astonished by the speed of the Soviet advance.

Like Operation *Uranus* a year before, the Red Army had launched a major attack where it was not expected and Rybalko's armour was moving faster than the Germans could react. By 5 November, Hoth knew that Vatutin had achieved a major success in breaking out from the Lyutezh bridgehead and realised that he had to choose what to save – either his 4.Panzerarmee or Kiev. Since Hoth knew that 25.Panzer-Division was en route from Germany and would detrain at Fastov, he ordered 7.Panzer-Division to move to defend the train station there instead of defending the approaches to Kiev. Likewise, he ordered 8.Panzer-Division to delay Soviet efforts to advance westwards along the rail lines to Zhitomir, another important logistics base. The only force left in Kiev was the depleted 75.Infanterie-Division, belonging to VII Armeekorps. Amazingly, the Germans had not yet destroyed the main rail bridge over the Dnepr in Kiev and VII Armeekorps was primarily focused on holding this area, not shifting forces to deal with the threat from the north, so Soviet troops were able to pour into the city late on 5 November.

Von Manstein continued his counter-offensive in early December 1943, hoping to cripple Vatutin's best tank units. However after weeks of continued operations, it was the German armour that was worn down. Here, a column of Panther tanks advance along a snow-covered road. (Nik Cornish at www.Stavka.org.uk)

A Soviet motorised rifle company boldly headed towards the city centre on the morning of 6 November, while another assault unit moved to capture the rail bridge intact. The VII Armeekorps did succeed in blowing up the bridge in time, but Soviet flags were soon appearing on buildings and it was clear that the city was lost. The VII Armeekorps abandoned Kiev post-haste and the Red Army marched in to liberate the city. The rapid loss of Kiev humiliated both von Manstein and Hoth and it demonstrated that Hitler's intent to use the Dnepr as a defensive bulwark had completely failed. Adding insult to injury, Rybalko's armour continued to advance rapidly, moving through Vasyl'kov to capture Fastov on 7 November before 7.Panzer-Division could establish a defence around the town. Hoth's left and centre recoiled back from the Dnepr in order to protect the line of communications, but his right flank – XXIV Panzerkorps – managed to maintain its hold on the Dnepr and the Bukrin bridgehead.

Von Manstein knew that powerful armoured reinforcements were en route to Heeresgruppe Süd from the West, including the veteran 1.SS-Panzer-Division Leibstandarte SS Adolf Hitler and 1.Panzer-Division as well as the inexperienced 25.Panzer-Division from Norway. Another new unit en route was schwere Panzer-Abteilung 509 equipped with Tiger I tanks. Altogether, these reinforcements possessed 558 tanks, including 172 Panthers and 72 Tigers. Prior to the Soviet breakout from the Lyutezh bridgehead, most of these reinforcements were earmarked for 8.Armee in Kirovograd, but now they were assigned to General der Panzertruppen Heinrich Eberbach's XXXXVIII Panzerkorps and ordered to concentrate at Bila Tserkva and Berdichev by 10 November. However, Rybalko's capture of Fastov threatened the use of the rail facilities at Bila Tserkva and Berdichev so Hoth realised that he needed a steady unit to act as a covering force. On 6 November, 'Das Reich' began pulling out of the line at Bukrin and transferred to Bila Tserkva; when they arrived there, the Waffen-SS troops were stunned to find Wehrmacht rear-area personnel evacuating the town in panic. The vanguard units of 'Das Reich' quickly stabilised the situation in the town and sent a tank company with seven Tigers and just eight infantrymen northwards in a movement to contact. Visibility was poor due to a mix of snow and drizzling rain. South-east of Fastov, the Tigers encountered six T-34s and knocked them out, but were forced to fall back as masses of Soviet troops appeared. Gradually, as more of 'Das Reich' arrived on 8 November, it was able to form a solid defence north of Bila Tserkva which protected 25.Panzer-Division as it detrained.

Hoth wanted time to detrain and assemble these powerful reinforcements for a proper counter-offensive, but he was instead forced to conduct piecemeal attacks to prevent 7th Guards Tank Corps from overrunning the XXXXVIII Panzerkorps assembly areas. Generalleutnant Adolf von Schell's 25.Panzer-Division, which had no prior combat experience, was committed virtually as it was offloaded. The LSSAH and 1.Panzer-Division were already in the process of unloading near Kirovograd and were forced to road-march north to Berdichev along very muddy roads, so they would not be available until 14 November. In order to hold off Rybalko's 3rd Guards Tank Army, 'Das Reich', Kampfgruppe von Wechmar from 25.Panzer-Division and a company from schwere Panzer-Abteilung 509 staged several local counter-attacks towards Fastov. In its first action, Kampfgruppe von Wechmar panicked when attacked by T-34s and retreated in disorder, suffering heavy losses of

Breakout from the Lyutezh bridgehead and the liberation of Kiev, 3–7 November 1943.

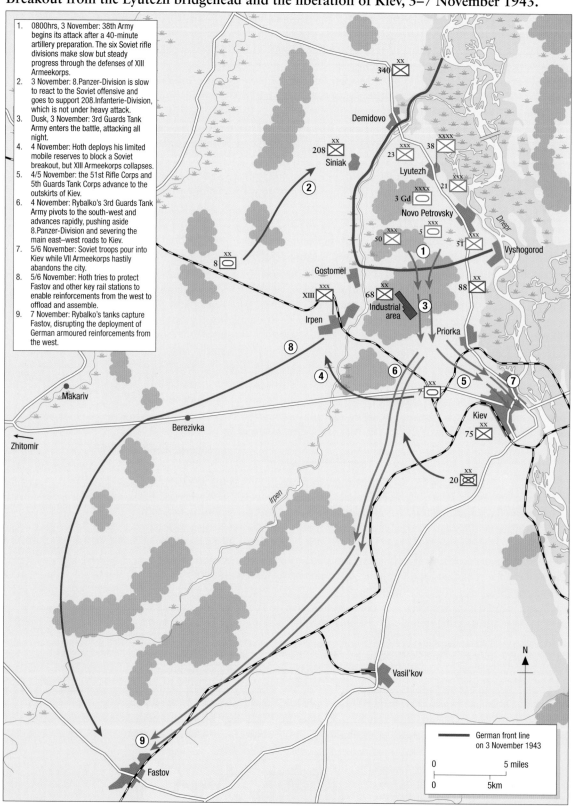

1. 0800hrs, 3 November: 38th Army begins its attack after a 40-minute artillery preparation. The six Soviet rifle divisions make slow but steady progress through the defenses of XIII Armeekorps.

2. 3 November: 8.Panzer-Division is slow to react to the Soviet offensive and goes to support 208.Infanterie-Division, which is not under heavy attack.

3. Dusk, 3 November: 3rd Guards Tank Army enters the battle, attacking all night.

4. 4 November: Hoth deploys his limited mobile reserves to block a Soviet breakout, but XIII Armeekorps collapses.

5. 4/5 November: the 51st Rifle Corps and 5th Guards Tank Corps advance to the outskirts of Kiev.

6. 4 November: Rybalko's 3rd Guards Tank Army pivots to the south-west and advances rapidly, pushing aside 8.Panzer-Division and severing the main east–west roads to Kiev.

7. 5/6 November: Soviet troops pour into Kiev while VII Armeekorps hastily abandons the city.

8. 5/6 November: Hoth tries to protect Fastov and other key rail stations to enable reinforcements from the west to offload and assemble.

9. 7 November: Rybalko's tanks capture Fastov, disrupting the deployment of German armoured reinforcements from the west.

German front line on 3 November 1943

0   5 miles

0   5km

men and vehicles. Von Schell was relieved of command. Overall, these local counter-attacks slowed Rybalko's advance but they proved very costly. Hoth claimed that Rybalko lost over 30 tanks in several days of skirmishing, but schwere Panzer-Abteilung 509 lost 7 Tiger Is destroyed, and only 14 were still operational after a few days of combat. By 11 November, 'Das Reich' had established a front north of Bila Tserkva and 1.Panzer-Division and LSSAH had arrived there. Yet just as Hoth was stabilising his centre, his left gave way.

After taking Kiev, Vatutin's 1st Ukrainian Front was not logistically prepared to mount a pursuit in all sectors, which enabled Hoth's broken left wing to retreat and coalesce around the supply centres at Zhitomir and Korosten. While Rybalko was fully focused on pushing southwards to Bila Tserkva, the only force available to advance due west into the vacuum left by the retreating Germans was the 23rd Rifle Corps from Moskalenko's 38th Army and General-leytenant Viktor K. Baranov's 1st Guards Cavalry Corps. Baranov's corps was actually a mixed armoured-cavalry force with over 100 tanks and some motorised infantry. Frölich's 8.Panzer-Division tried to defend Zhitomir, but was pushed out by Baranov on 13 November. The capture of Zhitomir was a catastrophe for Heeresgruppe Süd because the loss of this vital rail junction disrupted the flow of supply trains from the west. Von Manstein was forced to order Hoth to shift 1.Panzer-Division and the LSSAH westwards to deal with Baranov's cavalry group, instead of Rybalko's armour.

The day before XXXXVIII Panzerkorps was about to begin its counter-offensive, Hitler intervened by replacing Eberbach with General der Panzertruppen Hermann Balck, just returned from a month at the Salerno front in Italy. On 15 November, the LSSAH and 1.Panzer-Division attacked

Soviet infantry fighting their way into the suburbs of Kiev. Soviet assault groups reached the city before the Germans could react to block them. (Author's collection)

north towards the Kiev–Zhitomir road, with 'Das Reich' and 25.Panzer-Division protecting their right flank. The 7.Panzer-Division screened the left flank. Mud and rainy weather hindered the German advance, but XXXXVIII Panzerkorps slowly advanced, grinding up Baranov's overextended corps and parts of 38th Army. Both sides' supply situation was poor, with units frequently running out of fuel. On 20 November, the 7. and 8.Panzer divisions had nearly encircled Zhitomir, so Baranov abandoned the city and retreated before the pincers closed. Four days later, the XXXXVIII Panzerkorps pincers began to close around Brusilov, in an effort to trap some of Rybalko's armour. A series of close-range tank battles were fought in this heavily wooded area and the Germans encountered some of the new KV-85 heavy tanks in this sector. Introduced as an interim design until the IS-2 heavy tank was ready, the KV-85 was intended to counter the German Panther tank. When the pincers closed at Brusilov, the Germans claimed to have destroyed over 150 Soviet tanks, but most of Rybalko's armour escaped. The XXXXVIII Panzerkorps was exhausted, so von Manstein decided to pause the counter-offensive.

While the recapture of Zhitomir and Brusilov was helpful, Rybalko still held Fastov and Vatutin was pushing additional forces across the Dnepr to reinforce this sector. The German counter-offensive had not crushed any major Soviet units and had only retaken a small amount of terrain. Hitler had already decided to relieve Hoth for losing Kiev but had waited until after the counter-offensive ended. General der Panzertruppe Erhard Raus was given command of 4.Panzerarmee and ordered to renew the counter-offensive in early December. Hitler was still under the illusion that 4.Panzerarmee could crush Vatutin's forces west of Kiev and retake the city, although von Manstein knew that with limited supplies and Luftwaffe support, only tactical victories were now possible. Yet even as the Germans retook Zhitomir and Brusilov, powerful reinforcements were en route to Vatutin's 1st Ukrainian Front and he intended to conduct his own offensive in December.

A German StuG III assault gun, probably from Sturmgeschütz-Abteilung 202, abandoned in a forest near Kiev after the Soviet breakout from the Lyutezh bridgehead. (Author's collection)

NOVEMBER: BATTLES IN THE SOUTH

While Vatutin was advancing westwards from Kiev, the other three Soviet fronts were still struggling to get across the Dnepr in strength and reach their operational objectives. On 5 November, Stavka directed Konev's 2nd Ukrainian Front and Malinovsky's 3rd Ukrainian Front to cooperate on crushing the 1.Panzerarmee's forces around Krivoi Rog, while Tolbukhin's 4th Ukrainian Front eliminated the two German corps in the Nikopol bridgehead. However, German resistance in the south proved far more tenacious than expected.

Despite being rebuffed by Schörner's counter-attack, Konev intended to make another direct push towards Krivoi Rog with his 37th and 57th armies and 7th Guards Army, supported by Rotmistrov's 5th Guards Tank Army (18th Tank Corps, 29th Tank Corps, 5th Guards Mechanised Corps and 7th Mechanised Corps). Rotmistrov still had 323 tanks and 35 self-propelled guns available and the 1st Mechanised Corps and 20th Tank Corps would also be available for the breakthrough battle. Konev intended to bash his way through LII Armeekorps, which had two infantry divisions on the front line and SS-Panzergrenadier-Division 'Totenkopf' and the 11. and 23.Panzer divisions around Krivoi Rog. On 14 November, Konev began his offensive, with 37th Army compromising his main effort in the centre with six divisions, while the 57th Army and 7th Guards Army attacked on the flanks with 14 more divisions. However, ammunition was in short supply, so Konev's artillery failed to suppress the forward German defences. While 37th Army managed to push the German 76.Infanterie-Division back a few kilometres along the Inhulets River, the rapid arrival of the German tactical reserves prevented any breakthrough. The SS-Panzergrenadier-Division 'Totenkopf' and the 11. and 23.Panzer divisions completely blocked the advance to Krivoi Rog and limited Konev's forces to a 6–8km advance in a week of tough fighting. Having failed to achieve a breakthrough, Konev could not employ Rotmistrov's 5th Guards Tank Army in this sector.

Infantrymen from the 1st Ukrainian Front in the attack. Whereas the Germans were running out of infantry, the Red Army now enjoyed a large quantitative edge in this arm, which was also approaching qualitative parity with the German infantry. The liberation of the Ukraine enabled the Red Army to conscript thousands of fresh troops to replace its losses. (Author's collection)

Undeterred by this failure, Konev re-evaluated the situation and decided to shift his axis of attack from the south-west to the west, aiming for Oleksandriya. Since 1.Panzerarmee had massed much of its combat power around Krivoi Rog, this sector was only defended by Wöhler's 8.Armee with three infantry divisions (106., 167. and 376.) of XI Armeekorps and the much-reduced 6.Panzer-Division. Most of the German divisions were at half-strength, but Generalleutnant Arnold Szelinski's 376.Infanterie-Division, which had just arrived from Holland on 20 October, had almost a full complement of 15,000 troops. The original 376.Infanterie-Division had been destroyed at Stalingrad but the new formation had been organised during the summer and was one of the few full-strength infantry units available to Heeresgruppe Süd. Konev made General-leytenant Aleksei S. Zhadov's 5th Guards Army the main effort for his new offensive, which began under cover of a three-hour artillery bombardment at 0600hrs on 20 November. After the barrage lifted, VVS Il-2 Sturmoviks attacked the German artillery positions, then seven divisions from the 32nd and 33rd Guards Rifle corps surged forward, supported by two tank regiments. General-major Aleksandr I. Rodimtsev, one of the heroes of the defence of Stalingrad, led his 32nd Guards Rifle Corps against the seam between the 106. and 376.Infanterie divisions and achieved a 10km penetration. The XI Armeekorps committed 6.Panzer-Division and Sturmgeschütz-Abteilung 228 and 905 to try and plug the gap, but by the end of the day it was clear that Zhadov had shattered XI Armeekorps' front. Konev quickly decided to reinforce this success by transferring General-major Abram M. Khasan's 8th Mechanised Corps (with 123 tanks) and additional infantry to Zhadov.

Zhadov's offensive continued on 21 November and with the help of Khasan's mechanised corps was able to advance a further 6–8km. A large hole had been torn in the XI Armeekorps sector and only the presence of Szelinski's 376.Infanterie-Division prevented a complete collapse. Generaloberst Hans-Valentin Hube, now in command of 1.Panzerarmee, was

A German lFH 18 10.5cm howitzer abandoned near Kiev after the Soviets captured the city. The German VII Armeekorps made little attempt to defend Kiev and left a great deal of equipment behind due to lack of transport. It does not appear that the breech was even removed from this howitzer – indicating a very hasty retreat. (Author's collection)

forced to shift the 11. and 14.Panzer divisions to assist 8.Armee in containing the breakthrough. Konev upped the ante by transferring Rotmistrov's 5th Guards Tank Army, which joined the offensive on 22 November. Szelinski anchored the German defence in Oleksandriya, but Rotmistrov's armour bypassed the town and headed west towards Znam'yanka, while the 5th Guards Army pivoted northwards to roll up the XI Armeekorps position around Kremenchug. The 11.Panzer-Division clashed with the 18th Tank Corps north of Oleksandriya, but could not completely stop Rotmistrov's advance. Complicating the German effort to patch the breach, Rotmistrov sent a tank brigade on a raid into the German rear areas and eventually linked up with partisans. It was the onset of winter weather that slowed the Soviet advance and prevented a complete collapse, but as November ended Wöhler had still not repaired the rupture in his right flank.

As a secondary effort, Konev also attempted to cross the Dnepr near Cherkassy with elements of the 52nd Army. In mid-November, the Soviets were able to occupy some of the small islands in the Dnepr and use these as jumping-off positions for a cross-river assault. With the assistance of local partisans, the 52nd Army was able to seize a small lodgement west of Cherkassy in a heavily wooded area. The III Panzerkorps defended this sector of the Dnepr but apparently did not regard the Soviet bridgehead as a serious threat and simply cordoned it off. On 22 November, two Soviet rifle regiments and some tanks broke through the German corridor and advanced east to isolate 3.Panzer-Division inside Cherkassy. Chagrined by the Soviet success, the Germans were forced to request Luftwaffe aerial resupply for 3.Panzer-Division while bringing up SS-Panzergrenadier-Division 'Wiking' to assist in

A T-34 tank from the 1st Ukrainian Front enters Kiev with a squad of desant troops. Note that some of the Soviet troops appear to be wearing civilian items, suggesting that they are either partisans or recently conscripted. The Germans put up only a brief fight to keep the 38th Army out of Kiev, then evacuated the city.

reopening the road to Cherkassy. A combined attack by 3.Panzer-Division and 'Wiking' on 30 November succeeded in fighting through the Soviet cordon around Cherkassy, but the 52nd Army remained in close proximity to the city.

Meanwhile, Malinovsky's 3rd Ukrainian Front attempted to assist Konev's offensive towards Krivoi Rog by attacking towards the rail junction at Apostolovo with its 46th Army and 8th Guards Army, but 1.Panzerarmee's front was barely dented in two weeks heavy fighting between 14 and 28 November. A brief penetration by the 23rd Tank Corps was immediately shut down on 21 November by a counter-attack from 9.Panzer-Division. The German XXX Armeekorps and LVII Panzerkorps absorbed Malinovsky's blows and bled his assault formations dry. By the end of November, Malinovsky was running out of infantry and tanks and was forced to pause his offensive, having accomplished very little.

Likewise, Tolbukhin's 4th Ukrainian Front enjoyed no success against the Nikopol bridgehead, which was held by nine infantry divisions from 6. Armee's IV and XXIX Armeekorps. The terrain in this sector was marked by deep ravines, which favoured the defence by channelling enemy armour into predictable avenues of approach, which were mined. The 6.Armee kept 24.Panzer-Division in tactical reserve to support the bridgehead, and on 13 November, this division was used to mount a surprise spoiling attack against the 3rd Guards Army. The German tanks caught the 61st Guards Rifle Division by surprise and penetrated its sector, before turning around and returning to their lines. Although brief, this German attack unnerved Tolbukhin and he delayed his own offensive by a week. On 20 November, Tolbukhin finally attacked with the 5th Shock, 3rd Guards and 28th armies. Attacking behind a smokescreen, the 5th Shock Army achieved some success against 111.Infanterie-Division and then pushed the 4th Guards Mechanised Corps through a small gap in the German line. Over 100 Soviet tanks supported the attack. However, 24.Panzer-Division immediately committed two *Kampfgruppen* with 30 PzKpfw IV, 30 StuG III assault guns and 12

Churchill tanks from the 48th Guards Heavy Tank Regiment, 5th Guards Tank Corps, enter Kiev, greeted by civilians, November 1943. The Red Army employed Churchills in separate heavy tank regiments, using them as breakthrough tanks due to their thick frontal armour.

Ferdinand tank destroyers, which inflicted heavy damage upon the 4th Guards Mechanised Corps. Consequently, the 5th Shock Army was almost knocked back to its start line. On 26 November, Tolbukhin committed 19th Tank Corps in the 28th Army sector, but 24.Panzer-Division suddenly appeared on its flank and inflicted another stinging defeat. Amazingly, the German defenders in the Nikopol bridgehead repulsed the attacks of four Soviet armies.

DECEMBER: VATUTIN'S BREAKTHROUGH

At the beginning of December, there was a brief operational pause while both sides prepared to resume offensive operations. Von Manstein waited until winter snow hardened the ground for his tanks, then ordered XXXXVIII Panzerkorps to attempt a pincer attack on 6 December against a Soviet rifle corps from 60th Army holding the town of Radomyschyl. One pincer was formed by 1. and 7.Panzer divisions and 1.SS-Panzer-Division Leibstandarte SS Adolf Hitler while the other was formed by SS-Panzergrenadier-Division 'Das Reich' and 8. and 19.Panzer divisions. Fuel shortages and heavily wooded terrain hindered German mobility, which meant that it took four days for the pincers to close. Although von Manstein claimed that three Soviet rifle divisions had been destroyed, many of the Soviet troops actually escaped. Following this hollow victory, von Manstein wanted to use his armour to disrupt the Soviet 38th Army concentration near Meleni, east of Korosten. Vatutin shifted to the tactical defence, moving two rifle divisions and plenty of anti-tank units forward while pulling back most of Rybalko's 3rd Guards Tank Army to refit. Only the 25th Tank Corps remained in the vicinity of Meleni. Whereas von Manstein knew that he could no longer expect significant reinforcements, Vatutin received over 160,000 replacement troops in November and December.

On the evening of 18 December, the LSSAH division and 1.Panzer-Division attacked the 38th Army units deployed near Meleni, supported by 30 artillery batteries. The LSSAH attacked with 52 tanks, 18 assault guns and 12 Marder tank destroyers and its SPW-equipped Panzergrenadier-Bataillon led by the fanatical Sturmbannführer Joachim Peiper. Nevertheless, the Germans were surprised to run into massed anti-tank guns and mines, which limited their ability to advance. The terrain was also thickly wooded, which favoured the defence. Clearly, Vatutin had learned how to absorb a German armoured attack. Balck's XXXXVIII Panzerkorps attacked fruitlessly for three days, but it failed to encircle any

Soviet officers near a pontoon bridge over the Dnepr, late November 1943. The Soviet tactical bridging of the Dnepr was an amazing accomplishment and enabled the Red Army to mount multi-army offensives west of the river within a matter of weeks. (Author's collection)

Situation along the Lower Dnepr, late December 1943.

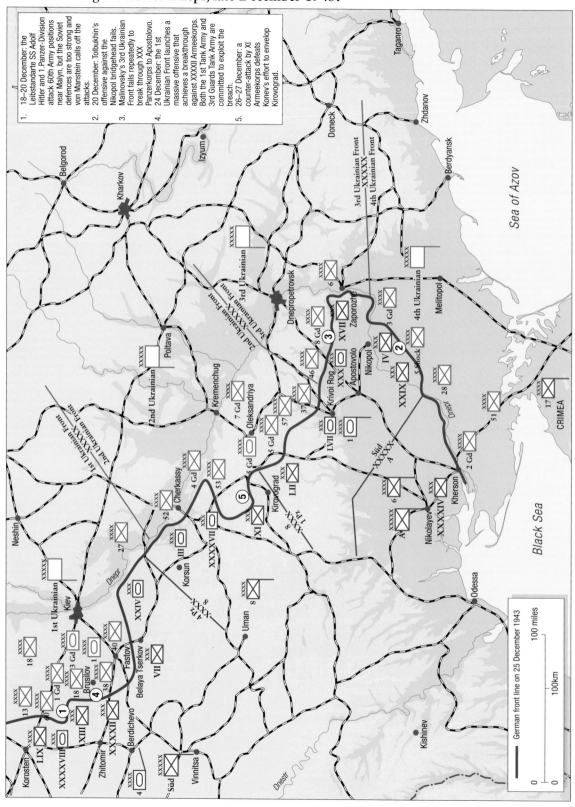

1. 18–20 December: the Leibstandarte SS Adolf Hitler and 1.Panzer-Division attack 60th Army positions near Malyn, but the Soviet defences are too strong and von Manstein calls off the attacks.
2. 20 December: Tolbukhin's offensive against the Nikopol bridgehead fails.
3. Malinovsky's 3rd Ukrainian Front fails repeatedly to break through XXX Panzerkorps to Apostolovo.
4. 24 December: the 1st Ukrainian Front launches a massive offensive that achieves a breakthrough against XXXII Armeekorps. Both the 1st Tank Army and 3rd Guards Tank Army are committed to exploit the breach.
5. 26–27 December: a counter-attack by XI Armeekorps defeats Konev's effort to envelop Kirovograd.

German front line on 25 December 1943

0   100 miles
0   100km

84

Soviet units and von Manstein was forced to end the operation on 20 December. Although the LSSAH claimed to have knocked out about 40 enemy tanks during the offensive, about 60 per cent of its own armour had been rendered non-operational, mostly due to mine damage. In sum, von Manstein's counter-offensives between 15 November and 20 December achieved only modest success and failed to destroy Rybalko's 3rd Guards Tank Army as intended. Von Manstein believed that he had inflicted great damage upon Vatutin's 1st Ukrainian Front and claimed that his forces had destroyed over 700 Soviet tanks in the counter-offensive, but it was his own Panzer divisions that were now much reduced. By 20 December barely 46 per cent of 4.Panzerarmee's armour was still operational. Five weeks of heavy combat had reduced the LSSAH from 218 tanks to only 19 operational tanks and 'Das Reich' had suffered such heavy losses that most of the division was sent to rebuild in France, leaving only a brigade-size *Kampfgruppe* with 4.Panzerarmee. Rather than the battle of Kursk, it was the Dnepr campaign that broke many of the best Panzer divisions on the Eastern Front.

While von Manstein's counter-offensive was engaging Vatutin's infantry and anti-tank guns, Soviet engineers rebuilt the bridges in Kiev in just three weeks. Once the bridges were repaired, Rybalko's 3rd Guards Tank Army received new tanks and fresh crews to replace his losses, restoring its combat capability. Furthermore, Stavka transferred Katukov's 1st Tank Army (4th Guards Tank Corps, 11th Guards Tank Corps and 8th Guards Mechanised Corps), which had 546 tanks and self-propelled guns, by rail directly to the west side of the Dnepr. Just as von Manstein's counter-offensive culminated, Katukov was assembling his army near Fastov. Now Vatutin had two tank armies massed for his next offensive, while 4.Panzerarmee's armour was stretched between Fastov and Korosten, with most of its strength shifted to its left. Vatutin intended to strike 4.Panzerarmee's weakened right flank, near Brusilov.

In order to concentrate armour for the counter-attacks against Radomyschyl and Meleni, Raus was forced to use his other Panzer divisions to conduct mobile defences along parts of the front. General der Infanterie Franz Mattenklott's XXXXII Armeekorps was holding a 40km stretch of front near Brusilov with the 8., 19. and 25.Panzer divisions because there was little infantry left in 4.Panzerarmee. Källner's 19.Panzer-Division had just 16

Von Manstein launched several powerful armoured counter-attacks against Vatutin's 1st Ukrainian Front in November and December 1943, but failed to achieve any lasting results. German armour attacked in low visibility conditions, resulting in short-range tank battles. (Bundesarchiv, Bild 101I-708-0299-01; photo: Scheerer (e.))

operational tanks and eight self-propelled Panzerjäger, while 25.Panzer-Division had 51 tanks and seven assault guns. None of Mattenklott's tanks were Panthers or Tigers.

Thus it came as a great shock for von Manstein and Raus when Moskalenko's 38th Army began a 60-minute artillery preparation against XXXXII Armeekorps at 0600hrs on 24 December, then attacked the boundary between 19. and 25.Panzer divisions with ten rifle divisions supported by 200 tanks. The 19.Panzer-Division had too few Panzergrenadiers left to mount a real defence and instead conducted a fighting withdrawal to avoid encirclement. Within hours, the center of XXXXII Armeekorps was collapsing under heavy pressure and 8.Panzer-Division began to retreat as well. Once it was clear that Moskalenko had achieved a tactical breakthrough, Vatutin committed both Katukov's 1st Tank Army and Rybalko's 3rd Guards Tank Army to exploit this – the first time that two tank armies had attacked simultaneously side by side. Altogether, these two tank armies comprised an armoured fist with over 700 tanks and self-propelled guns and enjoyed a 5:1 local superiority over Mattenklott's XXXXII Armeekorps. Both 8. and 19. Panzer divisions were soon surrounded and under heavy attack.

Although surprised by the scale of Vatutin's offensive, Raus shifted 1. Panzer-Division and the LSSAH division from Balck's XXXXVIII Panzerkorps south to secure Zhitomir and block the wave of Soviet armour and infantry. However, XXXXII Armeekorps was collapsing quickly and Balck's Panzers ran into a huge traffic jam in Zhitomir caused by retreating support units. Although 8. and 19.Panzer divisions were able to fight their way out of encirclement, Katukov and Rybalko's armour chose to ignore Balck's Panzers near Zhitomir and instead advance southwards into the gap between Berdichev and Bila Tserkva. In an effort to stay ahead of Vatutin's armour, Raus again shifted XXXXVIII Panzerkorps south to Berdichev, but left XIII Armeekorps to hold Zhitomir. Vatutin simply used his superior numbers to attack everywhere else along the front, pushing LIX Armeekorps back to Korosten and moving to encircle XIII Armeekorps in Zhitomir. Korosten fell on 29 December and by the next day 4.Panzerarmee had been broken into three pieces with large gaps in between. As he no longer had a continuous front, Raus was forced to abandon Zhitomir but he tried to make a stand at Berdichev and Bila Tserkva on the flanks of Vatutin's breakthrough in an effort to slow the avalanche. As 1943 and the Lower Dnepr campaign came to a close, Vatutin had achieved a major breakthrough and Raus' 4.Panzerarmee was in full retreat.

In Konev's section of the front, Zhadov's 5th Guards Army and Rotmistrov's 5th Guards Tank Army continued to grind westwards towards Znam'yanka, but were slowed by rain, snow and the fierce resistance of XI Armeekorps. The 10.

German troops stormed their way into Zhitomir on 20 November 1943 – their one significant tactical victory during the Dnepr campaign. However, the victory was short-lived and 4.Panzerarmee was forced to abandon the town in late December. (*Süddeutsche Zeitung*, 00010596)

Panzergrenadier-Division was firmly entrenched in Znam'yanka, but Rotmistrov was able to achieve a breakthrough on 5 December and encircle parts of 14.Panzer-Division. When the 7th Guards Army joined the offensive the next day, XI Armeekorps' front collapsed and the Germans were forced to abandon Oleksandriya. However, Wöhler's 8.Armee committed the 11. and 14.Panzer divisions to hold Znam'yanka and they went toe-to-toe with Rotmistrov's 5th Guards Tank Army for the next three days. Surprisingly, Rotmistrov's tankers prevailed in these actions and 8.Armee lost Znam'yanka by nightfall on 9 December. Wöhler's right flank had been ripped asunder and he was forced to scrounge for forces to plug the gap, which meant thinning out III Panzerkorps along the Dnepr near Cherkassy. The Soviet 52nd Army had continued to reinforce its bridgehead near Cherkassy and with Wöhler's 8.Armee in chaos, the 73rd Rifle Corps mounted a successful attack out of the bridgehead, which succeeded in capturing Cherkassy on 14 December.

Yet rather than continue west to smash 8.Armee, Zhukov redirected Konev to pivot 5th Guards Tank Army and 5th Guards Army south from Znam'yanka and proceed against Kirovograd. Although Stavka thoughtfully transferred two rifle corps from Malinovsky's 3rd Ukrainian Front to reinforce the new push, Rotmistrov only had 164 tanks and self-propelled guns still operational and Konev's forces were nearly spent. In five days of heavy fighting, Konev's forces advanced 30km but there were no breakthroughs and by 15 December the offensive had culminated. Unfortunately, Soviet mechanised units were left overextended and vulnerable. South-east of Kirovograd, the 1st Mechanised Corps occupied a narrow salient. On 17 December, the German LII Armeekorps began a pincer attack against the salient with 11.Panzer-Division and 2.Fallschirmjäger-Division on the west side and 13. and 17.Panzer divisions on the east side. The 1st Mechanised Corps was badly mauled, but withdrew in time to avoid destruction. The 5th Guards Mechanised Corps was also disrupted by German counter-attacks and on 26/27 December the 3., 6. and 11.Panzer divisions succeeded in encircling and destroying a Soviet rifle division and a mechanised brigade. Thereafter, both sides were exhausted and shifted to the defence for several weeks.

Malinovsky's 3rd Ukrainian Front failed to achieve anything useful in December, but instead bled its front-line units attempting to reach Apostolovo. Hube's 1.Panzerarmee maintained a solid front between Krivoi Rog and Zaporozhe, yielding very little ground. Tolbukhin continued to attack 6.Armee's forces in the Nikopol bridgehead but the main attack on 20 December was a complete failure. Although Stavka allowed the 2nd, 3rd and 4th Ukrainian fronts a brief operational pause in late December, all three were ordered to prepare for a new series of coordinated offensives in January 1944.

A German Marder III waits in ambush outside Zhitomir, 14 December 1943. The weather had cleared, but the German armoured units were worn out and had to shift to the defence. (*Süddeutsche Zeitung*, 00010595)

FIGHT FOR SURVIVAL, CHRISTMAS DAY 1943 (PP. 88–89)

On 24 December 1943, Vatutin's 1st Ukrainian Front launched a massive offensive against 4.Panzerarmee's XXXXII Armeekorps east of Zhitomir and quickly achieved a major breakthrough. Vatutin then pushed the 1st Tank Army and 3rd Guards Tank Army into a 12km breach in the German front. Attempting a fighting withdrawal in the face of this mass of Soviet armour, the 8. and 19.Panzer divisions found themselves surrounded on Christmas morning. Balck's XXXXVIII Panzerkorps disengaged both the 1. Panzer-Division and LSSAH from combat around Meleni and dispatched *Kampfgruppen* from both to Zhitomir to rescue the two trapped German Panzer divisions. Frantic radio messages from the two encircled units indicated that they were virtually out of fuel and under heavy attack.

While XXXXVIII Panzerkorps was tangled up in a massive traffic jam around Zhitomir – created by retreating support units – the trapped and isolated Panzer divisions managed to break out of encirclement by fighting their way through wooded terrain.

Combat was ferocious and often fought at close quarters, with snow showers often limiting visibility to a few hundred metres.

In this scene, a mixed battlegroup from 8.Panzer-Division, including PzKpfw IV (**1**) medium tanks, SdKfz. 251 half-tracks (**2**) and troops on foot have run into a group of T-34s (**3**) and infantry (**4**) in a forest clearing during a snow shower, resulting in a point-blank battle. The snow has reduced visibility and muffled the sound of the approaching Germans. Fighting with the courage of desperation, the Germans manage to force their way through, but not without losses. Although both German divisions escaped encirclement, 4.Panzerarmee was soon broken into three pieces by Vatutin's offensive and ended 1943 in full retreat. Again and again, German units would become surrounded by the advancing Soviet pincers and have to fight their way out of encirclement. The defeat of 4.Panzerarmee effectively ended the Dnepr campaign and set the stage for the liberation of western Ukraine in early 1944.

AFTERMATH

The Red Army won a great victory in the Lower Dnepr offensive, but the price of that victory was over 1 million casualties, including 290,000 dead or missing. In addition, the Soviets lost about 12,000 tanks during the campaign. However, Soviet industry and Lend-Lease were able to replace most of their material losses in short order and conscripted liberated Ukrainians refilled the depleted ranks. In contrast, Heeresgruppe Süd suffered over 372,000 casualties during the Dnepr campaign, including 102,000 dead or missing. Most of von Manstein's Panzers were either destroyed or inoperative, leaving him with minimal mobile reserves. Due to Hitler's shift in priority to the West, Heeresgruppe Süd received fewer than 200,000 personnel replacements and insufficient tanks to rebuild its shattered Panzer divisions. Unlike earlier defeats such as Rostov and Stalingrad, there would be no 'bounce back' for Heeresgruppe Süd in the coming spring.

Vatutin kept the pressure on Raus' 4.Panzerarmee, and the 1st Ukrainian Front had captured both Berdichev and Bila Tserkva by 5 January 1944. Soon, Katukov's 1st Tank Army was threatening the main German supply base at Uman and von Manstein's headquarters at Vinnitsa. Konev's 2nd Ukrainian Front also continued to advance and finally liberated Kirovograd on 8 January. Vatutin's and Konev's forces gradually squeezed 8.Armee into a salient centred on the town of Korsun. Hitler refused to allow 8.Armee to retreat to more defensible lines, even though von Manstein warned him that it would be threatened with encirclement if either Vatutin or Konev achieved a breakthrough. In Hitler's mind, the propaganda value of retaining positions anywhere along the Dnepr was more important than the military value of conserving his ever-shrinking armies. Without permission from the OKH, von Manstein began shifting part of Hube's 1.Panzerarmee westwards to protect Wöhler's vulnerable 8.Armee. Yet Zhukov, Vatutin and Konev also recognised the vulnerability of the Korsun salient to a pincer attack and began planning a multi-front offensive to smash 8.Armee.

Not content to remain on the defensive and be pounded into dust, von Manstein opted to mount a counter-offensive against the spearheads of Katukov's 1st Tank Army on 24 January. This week-long operation inflicted painful losses on Katukov's armour and temporarily halted Vatutin's advance upon Uman, but proved to be only another tactical success. On 25 January Konev attacked the east side of the Korsun salient and quickly achieved a breakthrough, into which he sent Rotmistrov's 5th Guards Tank Army. Vatutin's forces also pushed in the west side of the salient and sent the 6th Tank Army to link up with Rotmistrov's tankers at the town of Zvenigorodka on 28 January. The joint Soviet offensive succeeded in encircling 59,000 German troops from VII and XXXXII Armeekorps in the Korsun pocket, including the elite SS-Panzergrenadier-Division 'Wiking'. Mindful of his failure to rescue 6.Armee at Stalingrad a year earlier, von Manstein quickly assembled the III and XXXXVII Panzerkorps to mount a rescue mission known as Operation *Wanda*, while the Luftwaffe conducted daily aerial resupply missions to keep the isolated troops from starving. Determined to stop Operation *Wanda*, Vatutin and Konev massed all their available armour to block the relief effort, resulting in a series of costly tank battles. However, Operation *Wanda* was stopped 7km short of a link-up with the trapped troops, who were forced to mount a desperate breakout operation on the night of 16/17 February 1944. About 27,000 German troops escaped the Korsun pocket, but the battle was a major Soviet operational-level victory that cost Heeresgruppe Süd six divisions and much of its remaining Panzer reserves. After the battle, both von Manstein's left and right flanks were near collapse and he knew that he had to retreat before more of his forces were encircled and destroyed. In the south, Malinovsky's 3rd Ukrainian Front and Tolbukhin's 4th Ukrainian Front conducted a joint offensive that began on 30 January and succeeded in forcing 6.Armee to evacuate the Nikopol bridgehead on 7 February. Although the Germans continued to mount a desperate defence, Krivoi Rog was liberated on 24 February. After this, the Wehrmacht could no longer stop the Red Army's inexorable march to Berlin.

Hitler's poor decisions and interference with tactical matters was a major contributing factor to German defeat in the Dnepr campaign, although the inability of German commanders such as von Manstein, Hoth and Raus to anticipate Soviet actions also played a major role. Simply put, the Germans failed to recognise that the Red Army was evolving into a much more capable opponent, able to employ combined-arms operations in large-scale, multi-front offensives. Soviet operational mobility was exploited to the full by commanders such as Vatutin, who had learned a great deal from earlier defeats. However, the Red Army failed to adequately plan and stage logistically to conduct major river-crossing operations across the Dnepr then conduct major operations once across the river. Consequently, the initiative gained by the success of the initial ad hoc crossing efforts was squandered by having to wait weeks for engineers to build pontoon bridges, which allowed the Germans to contain the first bridgeheads. This was a further lesson that the Red Army learned as a result of the Dnepr campaign, and Soviet commanders would become increasingly efficient at vaulting over water barriers in the remaining 15 months of the war.

A monument commemorating the breakout from the Lyutezh bridgehead and liberation of Kiev, located at Novi Petrivtsi, 25km north-west of central Kiev. (Author's collection)

THE BATTLEFIELD TODAY

At the time of writing, the ongoing Russo-Ukrainian conflict limits the opportunity for battlefield tourism in the Ukraine. However, there are a number of locations associated with the Lower Dnepr campaign that are worth visiting, mostly near Kiev. In particular, visitors should begin with the National Museum of the History of the Great Patriotic War, located along the west bank of the Dnepr in Kiev. Originally built in the Soviet era, this museum has been upgraded to reflect more of the Ukrainian viewpoint of World War II. Unlike many historical museums that are difficult to find, you can't miss this one, since it is topped by the 62m-tall Motherland monument. Outside the museum, there are sculptures of Soviet troops fording the Dnepr, as well as equipment and vehicle displays. Inside the museum, there are 16 halls covering World War II in considerable detail. Hall No. 3 covers the defence of Kiev in 1941, while the liberation of Kiev is covered in Hall No. 11. This is a professionally organised museum and offers tours in multiple languages, including English. The museum is normally open 1000–1700 every day except Monday and is accessible by Kiev's metro system. The museum website, www.warmuseum.kiev.ua, is one of the most user-friendly Eastern-European military museum websites the author has visited.

Just outside Kiev, the National Museum-Preserve 'Battle for Kyiv 1943' is located 2 miles south of Lyutezh. This is an older-style museum, but still worth a visit. The main exhibit is a large diorama focusing on the breakout from the Lyutezh bridgehead in November 1943. Outside the exhibit, there are displays of equipment, a large monument and restored trenches and dugouts. The Dnepr itself is considerably wider at Lyutezh today,

A Soviet-era monument in Kiev commemorating the role of Soviet sailors in the battle of the Dnepr. Other monuments highlight the role of partisans and other services as well. (Author's collection)

compared to what it was in 1943. Another area with monuments and exhibits is located at Novi Petrivtsi, which also boasts a collection of preserved T-34 tanks and reconstructed trenches. Although considerable fighting occurred around Chernobyl, the 1986 nuclear disaster there has closed that area off to battlefield tourism for the foreseeable future. In contrast, the area around the Bukrin bridgehead has changed very little since 1943. This is a rural area, but there are a few World War II monuments, mostly of the 'T-34 tank on a plinth' type. There is a memorial for the airborne landing near Kanev and inside that town Soviet armoured train No. 56 is on display in a public park. The Myshuryn Rog area is much the same, although the Dnepr near Kremenchug is closer to its 1943 appearance.

The areas around Dnepropetrovsk, Zaporozhe and Nikopol have less to offer in the way of battlefield tourism, due in part to post-war development. These are essentially industrial and mining cities, with few resources devoted to tourism. Dnepropetrovsk at least has decent hotels and has the 'Battle of the Dnepr' diorama (a Soviet-era museum) still open, but in poor condition. As usual in these older museums, there are no considerations for English-language visitors. Visitors hoping to see bunkers from the Panther–Wotan Line will be disappointed, since the line consisted of little more than fieldworks; there are thus few reminders of Hitler's 'Eastern Rampart' visible today.

FURTHER READING

Barratt, Stephen, *Zhitomir-Berdichev: German Operations West of Kiev 24 December 1943–31 January 1944* (Solihull, UK: Helion & Company Ltd., 2012)

Glantz, David M., *The Soviet Airborne Experience* (Fort Leavenworth, KS: U.S. Army Command and Staff College, 1984)

——, *Forgotten Battles of the German-Soviet War 1941–1945*, Volume V, Part Two (self-published, 2000)

Dunn, Walter Scott, *The Soviet Economy and the Red Army, 1930–1945* (Westport, CT: Praeger, 1995)

Haupt, Werner, *Die 8. Panzer-Division im 2.Weltkrieg* (Eggolsheim: Podzun-Pallas Verlag, 1987)

Hinze, Rolf, *Crucible of Combat: Germany's Defensive Battles in the Ukraine, 1943–44* (Solihull, UK: Helion & Co. Ltd., 2009)

Kumanov, Georgy A., *Voina i Zheleznodorozhnyi Transport SSSR, 1941–1945 (War and Rail Transport of the USSR, 1941–1945)*(Moscow: Nauka, 1988)

Kurkotkin, Semyon K. (ed.), *Tyl Sovetskikh Vooruzhennykh Sil v Velikoi Otechestvennoi Voine, 1941–1945 gg (The Rear of the Soviet Armed Forces in the Great Patriotic War, 1941–1945)* (Moscow: Voenizdat, 1977)

Malinovski, Gleb V., *Brigady Inzhenernykh Voysk Krasnoy Armii 1941–1945 (Engineer Brigades of the Red Army, 1941–1945)* (Moscow: Patriot Publishing, 2005)

Moskalenko, Kirill S., *Na Yugo-Zapadnom Napravlenii (In the South-West Direction)* (Moscow: Nauka, 1969)

Nipe, George M., *Decision in the Ukraine: Summer 1943, II SS and III Panzerkorps* (Winnipeg: J. J. Fedorowicz Publishing Inc., 1996)

Staskov, Nikolai V., '1943 Dnepr Airborne Operation: Lessons and Conclusions', *Military Thought*, Vol. 12, No. 4 (July 2003)

Tsirlin, Aleksandr D., P. Biryukov, V. P. Istomin and E. H. Fedoseyev, *Inzhenernyye Voyska v Boyakh za Sovetskuyu Rodinu (Army Corps of Engineers in the Battle for the Soviet Motherland)* (Moscow: Military Publishing, 1970)

INDEX